Victorian Pontypridd

and its villages

Victorian Pontypridd
and its villages

Don Powell

MERTON PRIORY PRESS

First published 1996

Published by
Merton Priory Press Ltd
67 Merthyr Road, Whitchurch
Cardiff CF4 1DD

ISBN 1 898937 23 0

Dedication

To my wife, Barbara, for her patience,
care and love through nearly fifty years

Printed by
Hillman Printers (Frome) Ltd
Handlemaker Road
Marston Trading Estate
Frome, Somerset, BA11 4RW

Contents

Acknowledgements

This book is a presentation of the life and times of Pontypridd and district during the long reign of Queen Victoria (1837–1901). To give a fuller picture of our heritage from the Victorian years, some reference is necessarily made to the years before and after the reign. Every effort has been made to ensure accuracy of the facts researched.

My grateful thanks are due to the former Mid Glamorgan County Libraries for the facilities accorded to me during my several years research of the Local Collection at Pontypridd Library; to the Chief Constable of South Wales Constabulary for providing facilities for my research at the South Wales Police Museum, Bridgend; to Mr Brian Davies, Curator of the Historical & Cultural Centre in Pontypridd, for writing the Foreword to the book; to Mrs J. Penny Pugh, formerly Librarian at Rhydyfelin Library and now Reference Librarian at Pontypridd Library, for her invaluable contribution to the book by locating many sources of information for research; to Mr D.J. Rees (Jim), in appreciation of his contributions to local history and for the many encouraging and interesting conversations we have had together on the subject; and generally to many friends for their support and to the staff at museums, libraries and elsewhere in South Wales for their help and courtesy.

Many of the photographs and other illustrations are from my own collection. For others, I am indebted to and acknowledge with thanks the courtesy of the Rhondda-Cynon-Taff County Borough Libraries, Local Collection; Pontypridd Historical & Cultural Centre; South Wales Police Museum, Bridgend; Valentines of Dundee Ltd; and my son Graham Powell for some modern photographs. I apologise to anyone to whom acknowledgement may be due but, inadvertently, has not been given.

Pontypridd   Don Powell
September 1996

Foreword

Don Powell has written a book which will surely be well received. Pontypridd of course has its historians, from Owen Morgan ('Morien') back at the beginning of the century, to D.J. Rees in recent years. Unfortunately none of their books is currently in print. This book more than fills the gap. It summarises the work of previous historians and adds much that is new.

This is a portrait of the town and its people, evoking character and atmosphere. It gives us an exceptionally useful account of the evolution of an urban landscape, street by street and building by building. I will use it, and I am sure others will also, as an invaluable guide to the history of the town's buildings and the successive generations who have occupied and used them. It brings to life the history of the community in a way that should encourage us to ensure that no more of our building heritage is unnecessarily destroyed.

In these pages the people of Victorian Pontypridd come to life in a series of anecdotes and character sketches, which prove how much fascinating social history there is in the files of local newspapers.

I am grateful to Don for asking me to write this Foreword, because I can use the opportunity to encourage others to follow his example. Pontypridd is a young town, which nevertheless has a fascinating history, much of which is still within living memory. Don has done the groundwork by providing us with a sound history of the town up to the beginning of the present century. I am sure that all who read this book will both enjoy and profit from it. I hope that some will be encouraged to put pen to paper and continue the story.

Brian Davies
Curator
Pontypridd Historical & Cultural Centre

September 1996

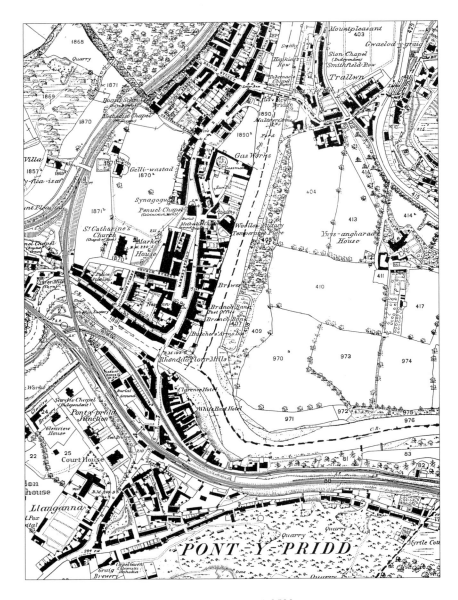

Pontypridd in 1875, from the Ordnance Survey 1:2500 map.

Prologue

Fog clung to the River Taff and the Old Bridge in Pontypridd as Charles Mitchell walked from his house in Morgan Street early on a Monday morning in September 1882. He turned down into Sion Street where yellow light from a solitary gas lamp glimmered on the row of cottages which faced the river. He was surprised to see a hansom cab, with its wheels skirting the edge of the bank, dangerously near to falling into the river and dragging the horse with it. The cab was deserted.

He led the horse to safety and examined the cab closely. The knee-doors of the passenger compartment hung open. A crumpled rug lay on the seat. The reins trailed loosely over the roof bracket. He called out and peered into the gloom of the riverside but there was no answering shout, no sign of life. Police took the horse and cab to stables at the White Hart Hotel on the Tumble for further examination while other constables waded into the river and searched the banks along Sion Street and Berw Road. Nothing was found.

The cab, owned by a Newport man, was driven up from Cardiff on the Sunday night and a guinea fare paid by Mrs Filippini, the wife of a Taff Street jeweller. Despite many rumours and police enquiries, the driver's disappearance was not satisfactorily explained. He never returned to his Newport home. Did he fall into the river and drown? Suicide? No body was ever found. Was he murdered and his body concealed? No evidence pointed to a crime having been committed.

The Victorians loved mysteries and tales of the supernatural. It was an age of gaslight, oil lamps and flickering candles which made it easy to see or imagine phantom figures in shadowy rooms, dark streets and dismal passages now spirited away by the bright lights of today. They knew the times of Jack the Ripper and the gruesome Whitechapel murders. No such dramatic series of events chilled Pontypridd with menace although, even here, the occasional murder or baffling mystery captured the headlines.

The reign of Queen Victoria brought impressive events such as the Great Exhibition at the Crystal Palace which displayed notable industrial and scientific progress. The reign saw things as diverse as the introduction of the penny post, crinoline fashions and the Charge of the Light Brigade. In darkest Africa, Stanley raised his hat to greet Dr Livingstone, he presumed. The queen celebrated her Diamond Jubilee in pomp and circumstance during the lives of important writers, poets, architects, artists and musicians. It was the age of railways, of I.K. Brunel and his feats of engineering, contrasts of life 'Upstairs and Downstairs', and the avidly read adventures of Sherlock Holmes. Everywhere there came swiftly moving change as industry spread its smoky towns and cities to make Britain the workshop of the world.

Pontypridd was busily adapting to its own significant changes: a growing population, commerce and industry, new mining villages, pits, pubs, chapels and churches, offices, schools and shops. Its people knew poverty and privation and constant hard labour to scrape together badly needed pennies. A heartening community spirit burned steadily amid comforting local achievements and appalling disasters. These things, and many more, made up the rich and fascinating heritage of Victorian Pontypridd.

Chapter 1

Shopping Basket

The lamplighter reached up with his lighting pole to ignite the burners of the gas street lamps in Market Street in Pontypridd. His hobnailed boots rang on the cobblestones of the quiet square as he strode in the shadows cast by the flickering yellow flame of each gaslamp in turn. Sometimes the gaslights in Market Street and Taff Street were left on all night as a protection against burglars and night prowlers and the lamplighter put the lamps out at dawn. But he usually lit them in the early hours of the morning to light the way on market days for the farmers who arrived in a procession of horse-drawn carts to unload their butter, eggs, cheese, bacon and meat for the stalls set out in a windswept, uncovered area where today's meat market shelters beneath its roof of glass.

It would be many years yet to the close of Queen Victoria's long reign and to the end of the nineteenth century which brought brighter street lighting to Pontypridd from the new incandescent 'mantle' lamps. The lamplighter could remember back before gaslight first came to Pontypridd in late January 1851 to streets in pitch darkness except for some places like the market approaches, which were illuminated by a few naphtha flares or an occasional oil street lamp.

Market Days

Pontypridd market attracted people of the town and surrounding valleys and visitors from all parts of the country. The Victorians, and later the Edwardians, flocked to Pontypridd in trains and horse-drawn brakes or buses, carriages, gigs, traps, hansom cabs and four-wheeler cabs. They came on horseback and in donkey carts to buy produce and goods at bargain prices from the market stallholders and town shopkeepers.

Cattle and sheep were sold in the present-day fruit and vegetable market avenue near its Church Street end. Early drovers to the town knew Church Street and Market Street together as Cattle Lane. There were no street stalls in the early Victorian years but, with the increasing

3

popularity and importance of the market, a Saturday indoor general produce market was introduced in 1887 in addition to the traditional Wednesday market.

There was an indoor market which sold mainly agricultural produce in Pontypridd as early as 1805. It was held for many years on the ground floor of a square-shaped building with an arched, stone-tiled roof standing in Market Square at the lower end of the now demolished Arcade and beside the stableyard wall of the one-time New Inn Hotel.

The Corn Market moved from Llantrisant in 1805 and stood until 1885 next to a corner china store, opposite today's Lloyds Bank. Its several entrances had imposing gates more than eight feet high. Sacks of corn, casks of butter, large cheeses and bales of wool were stacked there among ploughs, harrows, scythes and other farm implements. Farmers drove their cattle, sheep, pigs and horses to pens in the busy market avenue or to the small cattle market behind the Butchers Arms, later renamed the Park Hotel, now the premises of the Midland Bank and Woolworth's in Taff Street. There was also a cattle market near the now dismantled gasometer at the other end of town.

After a tramroad built by coalowner Walter Coffin in 1810 from his collieries at Dinas had linked with Dr Richard Griffiths's tramroad from Gyfeillon, near Hopkinstown, to his private canal at Treforest and the Glamorganshire Canal at Dynea, housewives from the Rhondda Valleys abandoned their perilous journeys on horseback or by cart across the valleys and mountain tracks to the old market at Llantrisant: they found it easier to travel to the markets at Pontypridd and Castle Court, Treforest, aboard several clean trams tagged on to the long trains of coal trams. The shoppers paid 3d to ride in the open horse-drawn trams and wooden platforms were built specially for them at points along the line. At times, they sat in pleasant sunshine glinting on their green valley as the trams rumbled along or they huddled from soaking rain beneath dripping umbrellas or shawls or shivered in bitter winds and snow. The route through Pontypridd and down to Treforest was called the Tramroad in Victorian times but is known today as Sardis Road and the Broadway—both wide because a turnpike road ran alongside the tramway.

The first market on the present Pontypridd site was held about 1850, the lessee being a Morgan Williams. It was comparatively small and fronted Market Street where the buildings of the Pontypridd Markets Co. offices are today. The Pontypridd Markets, Fairs & Town Hall Co.

was incorporated by Act of Parliament in 1877 and the lands of the old market place and buildings used as a market house, corn market, china warehouse and several adjoining shops, workshops and offices were purchased from Miss Clara Thomas and George William Griffiths Thomas. The first directors of the markets company were well known local businessmen Matthew Wayne Morgan, William Jones, William Williams, Robert Smythe, John Calvert of pit-sinking fame, John Jones, brewer David Leyshon, Hopkin Smith Davies, and Charles Bassett, Pontypridd's first postmaster, who was instrumental in 1856 in changing the prevailing name of the town from Newbridge to Pontypridd. David S. John is the present chairman of the Pontypridd Markets Co.

The market of 1888 comprised a large covered market where today's meat and butter markets are situated adjoining the Lesser Town Hall (now the new Clothes Market) built in 1885; a fruit and vegetable market (once the market yard but today the general market and actually the ground floor area of the New Town Hall built in 1890); and the avenue, an area which earlier had formed part of Gelliwastad Fields. The avenue extension, running to Penuel Lane and the Fountain area, was an uncovered place until partly roofed in 1929 and completed in 1932. It was originally a roadway along which horse-drawn hearses creaked their way to the graveyard of Penuel Chapel, built in 1860, which dominated the town centre.

Victorian market shoppers met stallholders such as George Mellor who came to the indoor market in the early 1870s. From his stall he sold best quality china which included some of the output of the Nantgarw and Swansea potteries. He came from Staffordshire about 1865 and set up a tallow and candle factory near the old slaughterhouse site on the Broadway. He also sold china from his marine store nearby before he opened his market stall and a shop in Market Street. His father owned a small pottery in Staffordshire where china was crated and sent by train to the Taff Vale Railway goods depot off Gelliwastad Road in Pontypridd. Customers bought everyday tableware from egg-cups to large cartwheel cheese-dishes then in fashion. For their mantelpieces, others took home pairs of Staffordshire china dogs with golden chains padlocked round their necks or ornament sets comprising two vases and a distinctive centrepiece. Gypsies bought up cheaper imported vases and peddled them in the new mining villages springing up locally. A brother, Walter Mellor, took over the business with the help of his wife Margaret and their sons and daughters until the business was sold in 1971 after a hundred years association with the market. Many market families continued a business down through the generations and some of today's stallholders follow ancestors who were themselves cradled in the trades.

The market was gaily decorated at Christmas with trimmings and candle lanterns. The whole indoor market scene was pervaded by the smell of faggots and peas—at one time cooked on an open fireplace which billowed smoke throughout the market hall. A dish of faggots and peas still retains its wide appeal in the market today. Children trooped round the market stalls (and the town and village shops) at New Year, hoping for a free lucky dip into a tub of bran or sawdust, or a gift of a penny or a halfpenny.

To recall the Victorian currency: 240 pennies or pence equalled one pound or the value of a gold sovereign. A sixpenny bit was known as a 'tanner' and written 6d. Twelve pennies made a shilling or a 'bob' and was written 1/- or 1s. The famous half-a-crown was 2s 6d. The pound or twenty shillings was written £1, while a guinea was 21s. A shilling became 5p in the new coinage in 1971.

Another early stallholder was Benjamin Rees Gibbon who came to the market in 1882 to help his mother to sell their Ystradowen farm produce. He sold butter at 1s a pound, eggs at 8d a dozen, cheese 6d a pound and best bacon at a pound for 9d. One stall sold plain and fancy Welsh woollens, serge, stocking yarns, and Welsh flannel aprons and petticoats: these were manufactured in a Graig factory owned by a Pembrokeshire man, Samuel John Jones. Umbrella man John Noble sold the wares he made in his Morgan Street workshop. In 1899 he was the only umbrella maker in east Glamorgan. Another man dealt in Singer sewing machines with treadles. Charles Coole sold mineral waters he made at Coedpenmaen and Charles Gaze sold sweets he made at Treforest, a big bagful costing a halfpenny. John Evans of West Street in Trallwn and George Watts made baskets in different shapes and sizes traditionally favoured by racing-pigeon fanciers, bakers, butchers and grocers.

But it was 'Roberts for baskets' of every kind made from cane or willow, and sometimes from hazel or mountain ash for use by local farmers. Mrs Francis Roberts opened a stall in 1895 (next to today's Copper Kettle cafe) with her brother Owen Morris. The baskets they sold included babies' layette baskets and Moses cradles for infants rocked to soothing Welsh lullabies. Many local anglers sat patiently beside a promising stretch of river on basketwork lidded stools from Roberts and, with any luck, plopped many fish into a Roberts creel. Frails, or rushwork baskets, were sold in ten sizes into which could be sewn anything from a small fish to a large salmon or pike; or perhaps a plump turkey or a selection of fruit. Francis Roberts also sold dolls and wooden toys and wooden or iron hoops. Hoops were favourite playthings for many boys and girls who bowled them with a guiding stick or a hooked rod of iron at speed along village streets. The basket stall was run later by her son, Bryn Roberts, who also took over the adjacent Mellor china stall in 1971. His son, John Roberts, runs the two stalls today although baskets are not now in great demand.

The meat market, in 1879 the site of a cart shed occupied by James Percy, was filled with stalls, clean and scrubbed white. The butchers and their boys were smartly clothed in blue-striped aprons and jaunty straw-boater hats. Three openings still lead to the Victorian Butter Market, also known as the Farmers Market and the Poultry Market until recent years. It also has an entrance from Church Street. The long, narrow hall had a row of tables along each side which overflowed with locally produced butter, cheeses, pots of cream and dressed poultry. The Butter Market lately had two long-fronted delicatessen stalls along one side with the Glenys Thomas cafe at the end. One stall was opened in 1937 by Mrs Kate Griffiths and run later by her son Billy Griffiths and his wife Elunid and now by their son Peter Griffiths.

Dennis Oscar Evans and his wife Gloria had the other stall. The family business started in 1847 when Oscar's great-grandfather, who was a founder of Saron Chapel in Treforest, came to the old Pontypridd market. Then, over 110 years ago, Oscar's grandfather, David Evans, came to the present spot in the Butter Market. He served as a member of the Pontypridd Urban District Council from 1901 to 1919 and was chairman of the council at the ceremonial opening in April 1909 of the White Bridge over the River Taff at the Berw. David Evans was known locally and at five other Welsh markets where he stood as 'Dai Black Pudding'. He discovered a tasty and unique recipe for the sausage-shaped delicacy and the secret, unwritten recipe has been passed down through the family. The art of preparation used by Oscar was included in an exhibition at the Museum of Welsh Life at St Fagans.

Above: The lower end of Taff Street in the late 1890s. The Butchers Arms (Park Hotel) is on the right (now Woolworth's and the Midland Bank). On the extreme left is the site of the present National Westminster Bank. The tall chimney stack in the background was Captain Williams's brewery behind Boots the Chemist. **Below:** Brakes or wagonettes in Market Street, looking towards the Fountain area, in 1899.

Above: General view of Pontypridd, *c.* 1900. The large building right of centre is the Royal Clarence Theatre (later the New Theatre and then the County Cinema), fronted by the original Clarence Hotel. Also seen is the tramroad along Sardis Road and down Broadway, then known as Tram Road. **Below:** The top end of town, *c.* 1950, showing the River Taff, Old Bridge, Victoria Bridge and the backdrop of Coed Craig-yr-Hesg.

Above: Market Street in late Victorian days, looking towards the end known as Market Square and the now demolished, earlier New Inn Hotel, which was replaced by the large red-brick building housing W.H. Smith and other shops fronting Taff Street. **Below:** A typical Victorian view of lower Taff Street with gaslamps and horse-drawn vehicles. The building on the left is now the National Westminster Bank site. Trees front the New Inn Hotel.

Above: High Street *c.* about 1950 looking towards Taff Street and the corner of Mill Street, showing the then fashionable windows of Marks & Spencer and other shops. The iron parapet of the bridge over the River Rhondda is seen on the left where the Mothercare store and others were built in more recent times. **Below:** A similar view taken in the late 1890s. The building protruding over the pavement on the right was the Temple of Fashion. On the left is one of the shops of John Crockett, on the corner of Mill Street (Walker & Hall's shop today).

Above: A street market in Market Street, *c.* 1950. **Below:** Fairs were often held in Market Street in Victorian and later days. This scene of the Easter Monday Fair in April 1933 features a typical carousel used in the street.

Above: Taff Street and Market Square, with Thomas Forrest Buildings (1876) in the centre. **Below:** Taff Street and the rear of Penuel Chapel, looking towards the Fountain area, *c.* 1890. Hopkin Morgan's shop, now the Prince's Cafe, is on the right. The C.G. Roberts's ironmonger's shop on the corner of the now demolished Gas Lane/Road is today partly occupied by Supasnaps. Further along is the Tea Exchange.

Above: The original New Inn Hotel building. Market Square is on the right. The hotel was a farmhouse in the 1730s before being rebuilt as shown. The New Inn was rebuilt again and extended in 1893 and demolished in 1981. **Below:** Penuel Chapel (now demolished) and the Fountain, 1899. The Town Hall is set back on the right.

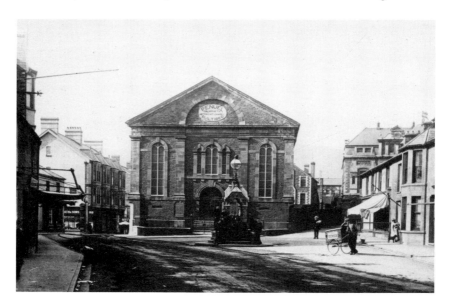

Outdoor Market

The Victorian Market bustled with shoppers in an atmosphere of banter and patter as it still does today. Rival traders shouted their offers to bunches of eager bargain hunters, curious onlookers, domestic servants from the 'upstairs downstairs' houses in the area, and the highly discriminating poor with shillings or pennies advanced by the Taff Street pawnbrokers. A trader holds up a fistful of goods: 'I won't ask you for ten shillings or even five ...'. His voice melts away into the babble of sounds in the market place. A pedlar played ballads on a concertina. Nearby, someone scraped on a violin as the sonorous peal of bells from St Catherine's church registered the happiness of a new bride and groom. Brass and silver bands of local collieries played at times in Market Square in front of the Arcade.

Many stalls in Market Street were covered by white tarpaulins with flying pennants or by striped awnings like peppermint sticks. Stall-holders satisfied endless needs for herbs, candles, clay pipes, bootlaces, whelks, metal polish, black lead, beeswax, leather goods, fly papers in sticky sheets and rolls, mousetraps, scrubbing brushes, toffee apples that drew wasps to their sweetness, egg timers, aspidistras in big jars, hair curling tongs, pocket watches, oil lamps, flat irons and cotton and woollen goods.

Little taller than the basket from which he dispensed his claimed cures or reliefs for bronchitis, consumption or tuberculosis, and other chest ailments was Tom Thumb the Cough Candy Man. Dressed in a white apron and a top hat, he stood at a corner of Market Square to sell his medicated sweets—and his shouts echoed in the tree-fronted New Inn Hotel (now demolished and replaced by the large, red brick building housing W.H. Smith and other shops). A quack promoted the reliability of his tooth powders by swinging a chair or heavy basket from his teeth. The Stocking Man swaggered through the crowds as he addressed them in Welsh. Hundreds of pairs of Welsh woollen stockings and socks, particularly favoured by miners, hung from a T-shaped piece of wood strung from his shoulders. Running into Market Square from the future Gwilym Evans corner shop and set high above the throng was a long plank supported on barrels. Along it scurried the 'Cheap Jack'. He banged his pots and pans together as he gave his eternal cry of 'Only a few left! Who'll give me ten shillings? Who'll give five bob? Come on, who'll say half-a-crown?' A dramatic clap of his hands would then seal a bargain for a shilling or a sixpence.

Often seen walking among the market crowds to visit nearby patients until his death and cremation in January 1893 was a controversial man with a large nose and a flowing beard. Dr William Price, the promoter of cremation, was instantly recognisable, clad in his green suit with red and white trimmings or in a flamboyant red robe with green sleeves, with a head-dress of a fox skin with the legs hanging over his shoulders and the tail trailing down his back. His dress contrasted sharply with the drab clothes of some men and the women's usually dark dresses, capes and bonnets. Some women dressed in skirts and blouses and straw boater hats or wore long dresses that swept the cobblestones; some wore the in-and-out-of-fashion bustle. Men turned out in three-piece suits with uncreased trousers and always wore caps or bowler hats while others wore blazers and boaters. A sprinkling of frock coats and top hats breathed elegance.

Conspicuous, too, was 'Grannie Cockles' who wore traditional Welsh costume. Many shoppers called at her pitch near the old Corn Market for a chat and to heed her warnings of pickpockets when they were about. Pickpockets risked imprisonment or birching when they ruined many a shopping trip to Pontypridd. Punishment for lawbreakers was harsh—even for the very young: typically, two boys discovered hiding in the market overnight after breaking into a toy stall suffered ten strokes of the birch rod between them. Three under ten-year-olds each received nine strokes on a day they remembered sadly for their enterprise in stealing fifty oranges.

Market Street

In Market Street shoppers threaded their way through crowds swarming in and out of the market, among the horse-drawn wagonettes or brakes arriving at the market approaches from Cilfynydd and Ynysybwl and the hansom cabs darting to and from all parts of the district, and among laden tricycles and bicycles and whistling errand boys hurrying here and there with their delivery baskets. Some shoppers made their way into town from the busy platforms of the Taff Vale Railway station on the Tumble or the Barry Railway station on the Graig—dodging the butchers carts speeding along High Street and Taff Street. Shoppers walked from the old Welsh Harp Hotel terminus at the top of Mill

Street after alighting from the horse-tramcars running between Porth and Pontypridd. They met the street-hawkers, the bell-ringing muffin man on the corner of the New Inn, the Shoni-onion man with his beret and his bike, and Tom Marshman's (Old Tom Cockles) cart.

Children were drawn irresistibly to Pontypridd's own Old Curiosity Shop complete with quaint Dickensian-style windows. Here, in a long demolished building near the Arcade, was a wonderland of rosy cheeked dolls with real hair, rag dolls, jointed wooden dolls. There were spinning tops, iron hoops, sailing ships, wooden engines and train sets and bowls of marbles of myriad hues. These delights competed with rubber balls, cardboard characters filled with sweets, acrobats on wires, lucky dips, toy brass instruments and drums. Months of pocket money was spent on Noah's arks, needlecases, paint boxes, trinkets, peep-shows and musical boxes.

The string of shops in Market Street often stayed open until eleven o'clock at night and assistants dared not take in the hams or hardware hanging outside before midnight on a Saturday, although by the turn of the century shop workers were calling for an eight-hour working day. Some traders flirted with the street for only short periods while others courted its attractions for decades: like Robert Smyth, chemist, wines and spirits merchant. He occupied his Medical Hall there from the early 1860s until he moved in April 1889 to his 'new and commodious buildings recently erected on the site of the Old Toll House in Taff Street' which were occupied later by Crosswell's off-licence. The buildings, on the corner of Turnpike Lane (also known as River Street and Ford Street), were demolished along with other shops and the Tredegar Arms to make way for today's Taff Vale shopping precinct.

There were familiar names in the street like Hepworth, Hodges, and Masters, clothiers. In November 1897 an application by the Public Benefit Boot Co. (later Lennards shoes) to the urban district council to run a cable from the Butchers Arms to brighten their new shop with electric lighting was refused, and all shops in the street continued to be lit by gaslight and oil lamps for several years. The centrally situated E. Hughes shop (later, Gwilym Evans) employed dressmakers on the premises to create gowns and other ladies' fashions. Edgar Fennell was the longest established fishmonger in Pontypridd and kept breakfast tables served with kippers at a penny a pair and supplied rabbits for a shilling, although he faced great competition from local poachers who stalked the woodlands and hillsides of the district with snares and guns and who snatched trout from the streams.

On chilly days, James Coombes's Cambrian Restaurant invited the cold and hungry shoppers with its blazing log fire and marble-topped tables spread with prime hams or large dishes of beef and plates of tarts and welcome cups of tea. The restaurant was a regular meeting place for the local trades council, unions and other groups.

Only a short step away was the Silver Teapot, a prestigious grocery store and cafe owned by Richard Rogers. A large silver teapot jutted out from the roof and hung over the impressive frontage of the building at the Reserve Entrance to the market. The shop later became the Tom Jones ironmongery. It is now the Market Tavern of a new New Inn Hotel. Children loved the chance of an errand to the Silver Teapot to fetch a jug of black treacle or perhaps a small cask of vinegar, and a free slice of cake.

The Market Street shop of William Pegler, who had a branch shop elsewhere in town, was typical of many local grocery shops in 1884. Shoppers walked up to wide counters lined down to a sawdust sprinkled floor with biscuit tins fitted with hinged, glass tops so that the contents could be viewed and sampled. The spotless wooden counters were scrubbed daily with scalding water. Assistants weighed out tea from each new chest into stout blue packets or into tin caddies, ladled sugar with a horn scoop from sacks into small blue bags, and dug butter from large slabs before patting it into shape on a sheet of grease-proofed paper and weighing it on shiny brass scales with a selection of small weights. The smells from gaslights and paraffin oil lamps mixed with those from sides of bacon, hams, coffee, cocoa, a barrel of apples, strings of onions, and cheeses set out to be tasted and selected by customers waiting patiently for their turn to be served personally. Shelves were lined with an array of pickles and jams and tinned foods. And condensed milk—when deliciously spread on a hunk of bread, it stuck to the grimy faces and ragged coat-sleeves of many Pontypridd youngsters.

Thomas Forrest was a photographer in Pontypridd for nearly forty years. He took an interest in the newly developing art while he was employed at Brown Lenox chainworks at Ynysangharad and started a photographic studio in 1861 in Berw Road. His appointments book filled rapidly and in 1876 he erected a block of buildings in Market Street where he opened his Cambrian Studio at No 14, alongside the flight of wide steps down into Taff Street and opposite to the then main

Post Office building. He specialised in portraiture, landscape and architectural subjects and, with his sons, also undertook picture framing and supplied the new and exciting magic lantern apparatus. There was a photographic studio at the premises until recent years but it is now an optician's.

An iron weighbridge or weighing machine was sunk into the Market Street roadway and a brick weigh-house stood beside it on the small area adjoining the wide steps. Tolls were paid to the Pontypridd Markets Co. for weighing every sack or bale to be pitched or stored in the market. The toll was a shilling for weighing any loaded or unloaded waggon and 6d for a cart. At the inception of the markets company in 1877, the tariff of tolls and charges for livestock and every box, basket, sack or tray of goods brought to the market for sale was highly detailed. The weighbridge was removed and the weigh-house demolished in 1935 since when a pillar box and a telephone box have occupied the site.

Cambrian Lane, a market entrance roadway running beside the old Penuel Chapel, was known as Occupation Road. It was an appropriate name: many craftsmen worked from the 1840s in the little cottages and workshops there and in the bordering area where the New Town Hall was later built. James Bullock made boots and shoes in the 1860s and 1870s, as did Hezekiah Stephens who had earlier worked in Taff Street. A good pair of miner's boots cost 5s or more. James Bullock, who also made clogs used by miners, cut out the soles on a fast-moving, foot-operated press. A loop of rope kept taut by his foot held a boot firmly on his shaping last. Nails were taken from a blob of them in his mouth and tapped home. James Edwards was another boot and shoe maker in Market Street in the 1880s and later. His women's lace-up or high-button boots cost 2s 6d a pair and men's fashionable shoes cost 3s 11d. Cabinet maker and wood turner Charles Granger worked at his hand-operated lathe in a workshop in a courtyard off the street from the 1860s and later from Rickard Street on the Graig for more than thirty years. His output included table and dairy ware and utensils like bowls, platters and candlesticks. Pontypridd depended greatly on its own craftsmen and women and a host of them worked near the market area and throughout the town.

The Victorian architecture of Market Street is seen in the high buildings of yellow brick decorated with red brick patterns. The Co-operative Movement was attracted to the area and late in 1898 planned for a Pontypridd store—the residents of Ynysybwl already had their Society. The Co-op came to Market Square and eventually took over the whole of the Arcade until 1984.

Arcade

The construction of the Arcade was completed in 1890 and its charm added to the attractions of Market Square. The Chinese Tea Co., later Llewellyn Delaney's select hat shop and gents mercer, stood on the right corner of the Arcade across from James Coombes's bakers and confectioners. They welcomed shoppers to the Arcade's glows of gaslight and oil lamps that mingled warmly to the top end opposite the old police station in St Catherine Street.

A decade earlier, the site of the Arcade and an area behind the original New Inn Hotel saw scores of forges where blacksmiths and farriers played the hammer on the anvil in pursuit of their ancient craft. Tinsmiths busied themselves alongside manufacturing plumbers, nailmakers and other artisans. Widow Evans, the proprietor of the site, sold some of the output at her large ironmongery and hardware shop in Taff Street. The Arcade and all the Co-op buildings were demolished in late 1987 and the whole area behind Lloyds Bank towards Mill Street and bordering part of Church Street was cleared for redevelopment.

In the Arcade in 1890, Robert Davies was a notable picture framer and Thomas Evans was a watchmaker. The Arcade offered more sweets from marketman Charles Gaze in later years and Charles Coole dispensed soft drinks in Tuck's Temperance Bar. H.H. Gibson's window glinted with gold and diamond rings, silver tea-caddies, inkstands, snuff boxes, and mustard pots lined with delicate blue glass. Henry Hibbert, Pontypridd's largest watchmaker, displayed pocket watches in gold and silver with the fashionable Albert watch-chains which adorned Victorian waistcoats.

Joseph Noyes, established in the town in 1873, sold fruit and vegetables and Mrs Emma Preece served tea and hot buttered scones and Welshcakes in her refreshment rooms. A few doors away was the Express Dairy with its pure white counters, pails and churns of milk, pale gold blocks of Welsh butter and cheese, and eggs—'Brown or white, Madam?'—at a shilling a dozen selected from wicker baskets, large and white. To promote sales of their new season's tea, the London & Lancs. Tea Co. gave away with every 6d quarter-pound packet things like towels, scrubbing brushes, basins, fireside shovels, and skipping-ropes. They flavoured the appeal of their 1s half-pound packets with free coal buckets and scuttles, wrought iron kettles, crockery, cutlery sets or large mirrors.

Tobacconists George Hacker and John Rees urged all good Welsh pipe-men to smoke Prince Llywelyn Shagg while Woodbine cigarettes sold at five for a penny. Small boys often clustered round the shop doorways to ask smokers, 'Any cigarette cards, please Mister?' Albums were soon filled with the many sets of cards issued. Mrs Elizabeth Miles, landlady of the New Inn Hotel, ran an arcade wines and spirits shop. Samuel Horsfield's Music Warehouse stocked pianos, accordions, harmoniums, and brass and stringed instruments which were important in Victorian homes where entertainment had to be self-created. At Mrs Minnie Hanham's shop, ladies could try on a satisfying range of hats decorated with feathers or ribbons, straw-hats radiant with butterflies, or large flower-trimmed picture hats with turned down brims.

In Church Street, running parallel to the arcade and the market, James Miller kept the china store on the corner from the early 1860s until it was demolished in 1885 with the adjoining Corn Market. Evan Davies made watches and clocks in the 1860s as did clockmaker and harpist Octavius Davies. In the 1870s and later decades, Church Street was a thriving workplace for several printers, stationers and book-binders, including John Carlton Lowe, David Hopkin, and Charles Monk. They sold greetings cards of delicate art design and quality on which Victorians set a high value, china inkwells in leather-covered boxes, glass inkwells with long funnels through which the pen reached the ink, blotting paper in rainbow colours to soak up the inevitable blotches on papers, thumbs and fingers; and nibs that slowly scratched their way through the ages.

Town Shops

The shops in Taff Street were smaller than the brightly lit stores of today but were generally filled with great character. Much frequented was Otto Faller, the pawnbroker or 'uncle' at number 34 (later, Arthur Faller), where men's Sunday best suits were regularly pledged on a

Monday and redeemed on a Friday or Saturday for pressing in readiness for church or chapel services. The pawnshop was often the cheapest place to buy clothes, blankets, watches and jewellery, their previous ownership sacrificed by depositors unable to afford the cost of redemption. A quilt was often 'popped' for half-a-crown which was spent next door in Chappell's Pork Shop. Part of the cash sometimes found its way to the Tredegar Arms across the road.

The tinkling doorbell at W. Stickland's sweetshop was an 'Open Sesame' to delight for children. A penny could buy about four ounces of sweets, and paper bags burst with bull's eyes, gobstoppers and lollipops, bootlaces of liquorice and clumps of creamy Everton toffee. Close by, the Pontypridd Toy Warehouse bulged with toys and fancy goods on a site afterwards enchanted by the Palladium cinema, now the Gateway supermarket. Crossbrook Music Stores had premises now occupied by A.T. Mays Travel and Servini's cafe on the corner of Crossbrook Street by the YMCA, built in Edwardian years. Several brooks running from Lanwood to the River Taff gave the street its name.

Berlin House stood at 52 Taff Street in 1889 (now the Iceland store) where E.M. Kuner sold a wide range of fancy goods. It included wickerwork shopping baskets, fire bellows, fender stools, dolls, parasols, painted gauze fans, and gloves long to the elbow. He also sold wools and silks for crewel-work, the design for tapestry making and embroidery which occupied many Victorian ladies for long hours. Isidor Kuner was a watchmaker and jeweller.

Several small shops linked the way to the Fountain area, known as Penuel Square and dominated by the chapel, which was demolished in 1967 and the graveyard removed to allow building of the Fraternity Parade where British Gas showroom, Abbey National and other shops are situated. The unveiling of the Fountain in 1895 by its donor Sir Alfred Thomas, Member of Parliament for East Glamorgan, created a popular venue for Temperance and other speakers. The Pontypridd Urban District Council, formed in that year, had its first offices at 56 Taff Street, now John Frazer, the tailors.

One of several hatters in the square was J.S. Evans, 'the People's Hatter', who sold the noted 'Challenge' hats at 3s to 4s each. The tall windows were crammed with shirts, loose collars, cravats, and many styles of cap for golfers and cyclists. At Cook's Fountain Toilet Saloon for men, hair was cut short. Men who let their hair grow long were faced with jibes of 'Poet!' or 'Musician!'. Heavy moustaches were common but hair oils were frowned upon.

Opposite the Fountain at No 16 was the bicycle depot of Morris Brothers who made and repaired cycles at their Ynysangharad Road workshop from 1878. Throughout ensuing years, they manufactured the 'boneshaker' bicycles which lacked pneumatic tyres, tricycles for one or two riders, and penny farthings. By 1898 when a cycling craze swept the country, their Cambrian safety bicycles sold for £14 and standard bicycles for £10. Before the introduction of chain guards for bicycles, ladies faced the problem of preventing entanglement of their long skirts in the chain and sprocket wheel and for some years knickerbocker suits and leggings found national favour with Victorian lady cyclists. When a skirt, short coat and blouse returned as cycling costume, the skirt was weighted with lead shot to prevent its blowing up and indecorously exposing an ankle to the rider's embarrassment.

Across the road and nearer to Penuel Chapel, the Tea Exchange traded for many years until the 1890s. Next door, in a building now occupied by the TSB, were some grocers and butchers with the Conservative Club overhead. Late in 1899, Thomas and Evans of Porth bought the shops and also opened a branch at Pontshonnorton. A family grocery business, Thomas and Evans prospered at many shops in the Rhondda Valley and were famed as the manufacturers of Corona Aerated Water or 'pop'. At the turn of the century they sold lard and margarine at 5d a pound, butter at 9d and Wiltshire bacon at 10d. During the Taff Vale Railway strike of 1900, they used a large steam-driven traction engine to haul cartloads of drinks from Porth to Pontypridd and Cardiff. The vibration that the engine caused in Taff Street shops brought many complaints: at one UDC meeting a councillor proposed that the T. and E. monstrosity be banned from the town because it shook bottles on chemists shelves violently. No action was taken after another councillor retorted: 'Chemists have no real cause for complaint, anyway. They keep telling us that the stuff on their shelves should be shaken before taken!'.

By one corner of Gas Lane where Supasnaps is today (earlier, Alexandre Fifty Shilling Tailors) C.G. Roberts's general ironmongery carried the largest and most varied stock in the valleys. The shop provided a range of steel hatchets for miners and tools for masons, carpenters and engineers, as well as dairy utensils, agricultural tools and machinery. For the home it stocked brass stair-rods and Roman helmet coal-scuttles, warming-pans, scales with brass or iron weights, black metal or brass fireplace fenders, tin baths for every miner's kitchen, flat irons and their trivet-like stands in cast brass, mangles, washtubs and scrubbing brushes, and washboards for knuckle-skinning drudgery. Earlier, from about 1860 to about 1880, the shop belonged to Evan Llewellyn, a nailmaker. Through his open door, passers-by could watch the nailmakers at their tiny forges and operating their foot-sledges. Large and small nails were hand made and every nail separately forged from a thin rod of iron.

Further down Taff Street, many cottages were private houses until late Victorian times. Local choirs rehearsed in the Assembly Rooms at the rear of Heath & Sons' piano shop at No 70. Nearby, Eugene Bauman, jeweller and watchmaker, was one of the oldest established traders in Pontypridd. Ladies were attracted to his wrist watches which originated about 1890 and were known then as bracelet watches. They were thought too effeminate to appeal to men. Another well known jeweller and watchmaker in the 1860s was Francis Joseph Kaltenbach. Oliver's shoeshop was at No 73 (now the Britannia Building Society) and at No 74 (Prince's Restaurant) was Hopkin Morgan's original shop where he sold bread and confectionery baked at his East Street, Trallwn, bakery. A four-pound loaf or quartern cost 4d.

Boots the Chemist opened a shop in March 1897 at 83 Taff Street on a site now dwarfed by their modern store. Besides perfumes and pure drugs, lines of the day included Boots Liver Pills, shuddering cod liver oil, Gratton's eye-watering embrocation for chills and sore throats, and Wills Hygeia health salts. Boots also stocked powerful horse and cattle medicines and the local farmers were confident that their off-colour animals would soon be galloping round the fields without a vet in sight.

The Victorians certainly joined in the spirit of local events: in the summer of 1899, Boots' offer of a free distribution of Doan's backache and kidney pills created such huge response that four police constables regulated a chaos of horses hooves and jostling crowds in Taff Street. People who looked gloomy or strained when they entered the shop apparently emerged within minutes all aglow. One instantly revived and rejuvenated pilgrim gasped, 'Those pills are dynamite!' Jesse Boot, the founder of the company, later started a countrywide 'shilling subscription' in aid of wounded British soldiers and the widows and orphans of men killed in the South African Boer War of 1899–1902. Starting with his donation of a thousand shillings (£50) the fund grew quickly and staff at the Pontypridd shop contributed a commendable 8s.

Lipton's opened a shop next door in November 1897 and offered large Christmas cakes at 4½d each, hams at 7d a pound and tea at a dramatically low price of 1s 7d a pound packed into free decorated tea caddies. The urban district council placed one of the new incandescent burner gaslights outside the shop. Shoppers contrasted its brilliance that Christmas with the pools of yellow light from lanterns in a Christmas card Market Square glistening with frost beneath bright stars as carollers, accompanied by the Treforest Corps Salvation Army Band, sang of herald angels, shepherds and kings. Some of today's joyful singers and musicians know the wonder of those merry ghosts of Christmas Past when the Christmas tree goes up every year outside the National Westminster Bank.

Other busy shops at this time were Home & Colonial, Scudamore (who had an ice-chamber for meat refrigeration) and Bracchi Brothers' cafe. W.H. Key, a dental surgeon and 'People's Chemist', retired in 1900 from his practice at 90 Taff Street, now Timpson's shoe shop adjoining Barclays Bank. As well as selling whisky and brandy at 2s 3d a bottle, William Key knew a busy trade in his penny Merlin headache powders. Thompson and Shackell's Music Saloon was built in 1890 on the corner of Taff Street and Market Square, a large building partly occupied later by Gwilym Evans's drapery store. At one time, grocer Griffith Evans was at 1 Taff Street at the corner with Mill Street and John Crockett's shops were at Nos 2 and 3 which are now all part of the National Westminster Bank premises. John Crockett was a prominent citizen and a partner of the Penygraig Coal Co. The shops were jewellers, pawnbrokers and ironmongers. They were highly reputable cabinet makers, upholsterers and polishers who could supply cradles for the new born and shrouds and coffins for the not so fortunate, as well as hearses drawn by black horses. The upper floors of the present bank housed the famous Victorian Cloth Hall, a large drapery, general outfitting and hat and cap warehouse. All branches of tailoring were carried out on the premises owned before the 1870s by Maria Jones and afterwards by John Daniel Jones.

In Victorian times the High Street leading to the Tumble was linked to Taff Street by the present River Rhondda bridge which had iron parapets allowing views of the river. The shop on the corner of the lower entrance to Ynysangharad Park (now Just Rentals with the old offices of the *Pontypridd Observer* above) was in 1897 the new 'Temple of Fashion' of Thomas Evans and, later, of John Evans. It extended out where the pavement curved and widened just opposite Mill Street and narrowed the access to the High Street. Windows showing the latest creations in cloaks, costumes and tea gowns drew many window shoppers but the protrusion of the building caused a traffic bottleneck which led to its demolition.

In the High Street was the M. Davies Art Depot which sold fine wools and silks. J.E. Brooks, hairdresser and tobacconist, was at No 4 where a haircut cost 3d and patrons could also take hot and cold baths. Brooks sold choice brand cigars at 18s for a box of 100, quarter-pound tins of tobacco for 1s 2d, and boxes of 100 May Blossom and Myrtle Grove cigarettes at 2s each. Henry Hibbert, the Arcade jeweller and also an auctioneer, had a business in Clarence Buildings under the Royal Clarence Theatre, afterwards the New Theatre and eventually the County Cinema. Trays held wedding rings at 10s each or a selection of gold Albert pocket watches at £2 and in silver from 5s. Display cases shone with quality attractions for discerning Victorians: silver candlesticks, biscuit barrels and babies' rattles, silver spoons, sugar tongs and sifters, silver photograph frames and card and pencil cases. Spectacles for all were priced at one shilling.

James Coombes, the Market Street restaurateur, ran a coffee tavern next to the Half Moon Hotel on Station Square. Opposite the station was the City Restaurant, and also the shop of pawnbroker Phillip Joseph, well known by Graig residents. Intending travellers, including miners and their families emigrating to the USA to work in the pits of Pennsylvania, found their portmanteaus, trunks and travelling bags at the Southern Rubber Co. which started in 1877 at No 2 Tramroad, or Broadway.

On the corner of Mill Street and adjoining the River Rhondda bridge, now lined with Marks & Spencer, Burton's, Mothercare and other shops, John Crockett's warehouse stocked Birmingham and Sheffield cutlery in the early 1860s on the site now of Walker & Hall. Next door was Oliver Davies (later W. Oswal Davies), chemist and seedsman. On the site of the present Halifax Building Society was R.N. Shaw, a London tailor, who in the late 1890s cut riding breeches priced at 27s 6d and a wide range of liveries, clerical and athletic outfits.

Several solicitors set up in Mill Street in the mid-nineteenth century. The practices of several distinguished men evolved into that of Morgan

Bruce, late of No 49 today. At the rear of the building are old stables where Sir Gerald Bruce lodged his white horse on his arrival at the offices. In Mill Street, too, shoppers could buy woollen goods at the small factory of Evan James where the Welsh National Anthem *Hen Wlad Fy Nhadau* was composed in 1856. The factory fell into disuse towards the end of the Victorian era and made way, with other buildings, for the County Hotel and Restaurant, managed in 1897 by Henry Crane. The building was owned later by Joseph Sprague, a well known private accountant of Tyfica Road. Some local authority offices now occupy the building.

Mill Street bustled with craftsmen from early in Queen Victoria's reign. In medieval times it was merely a rough track to Llanwonno, passing Gelli Fynaches farm and the nunnery above Graigwen. With the coming of the railways in 1840, the Taff Vale bridged the River Rhondda close upstream from the River Taff and an arch on the northernmost bank near the old Welsh Harp spanned the road to the Rhondda Valley. The arches overlooked a water-mill in a field which until recently was the site of a council depot. Horses were turned into the field to graze near the mill-race while their owners went into the town and market. Afterwards, the shoppers could enjoy a hot meal prepared at the mill, at one time by Mrs David Williams, before collecting sacks of flour on their way home.

Back at the market, shoppers secured last minute bargains in perishable goods as the stallholders packed up for the day. Knots of weary errand boys, clutching empty baskets, trudged back to their Taff Street shops where some proprietors and staff scrubbed their counters white, swept up and sprinkled fresh sawdust on the floors. The lamplighter was often about his duties as the last market cart clattered over the cobblestones out of Market Square and the sound of horses' hooves died away.

Chapter 2

Water Ways

Glamorganshire Canal

When the road from Merthyr through Gelligaer and Caerphilly to Cardiff became inadequate to carry the growing output of the ironworks around Merthyr—despite improvements to the road by Anthony Bacon in 1767—several ironmasters obtained an Act of Parliament in 1771 for the construction of a turnpike from Merthyr through Pontypridd to Tongwynlais, where it would link up with an existing road from Tongwynlais to Cardiff. But the high costs of carriage later prompted the ironmasters to seek an alternative means of transport and an Act was passed in 1790 for construction of the Glamorganshire Canal.

Connecting tramroads along the upper length of the canal would give the ironworks a more efficient and less expensive means of transport to the sea at Cardiff. A narrow boat, attended by a man and a boy, could carry up to 24 tons of iron: to move such a load by road needed twelve similarly attended road waggons and large teams of horses.

Construction of the canal began in 1790 when several hundred men were engaged by the contractor Thomas Dadford (a pupil of the pioneer canal engineer James Brindley) in partnership with his son Thomas Dadford Junior and Thomas Sheasby. Skilled cutters and gangs of labourers dug the canal with picks and shovels. A navvy's work was dangerous and scores of men were involved in accidents during their twelve-hour working days spent in removing earth and stones and rocks before puddling the canal bed with clay, digging out the locks, and forming embankments. Stone was obtained from local quarries along the route to supply materials for the locks, bridges, wharves, cottages and stables.

The navvies worked hard, drank hard and played hard. Typical wages comprised piece-work at a penny a yard of average canal width plus 4s a day subsistence payment. The men always found themselves involved in uproarious drinking bouts and riotous fights on pay days. Their violent behaviour was reportedly a constant menace at Merthyr and in the sparsely inhabited neighbourhood of Pontypridd, as well as Cardiff, with a population of less than two thousand.

The canal was opened from Merthyr to Pontypridd in May 1792 and from Merthyr to Cardiff in February 1794. It was finally completed when an extension to the sea lock in Cardiff was opened in 1798. The canal cost £103,600 and the Crawshay family of Merthyr were major shareholders in the highly profitable venture that continued to pay the limited maximum dividend of 8% until 1874. In November 1883 Lord Bute bought all the shares.

The head of the canal at Cyfarthfa Ironworks stood 568 feet above sea level and, to overcome the difference in height, 50 locks were constructed within the 25½ miles of canal. After descending 160 feet through a series of 16 locks in a mile between Cefn Glas, near Quakers Yard, and Abercynon (then known as Navigation) the canal entered a basin on which a fire station was sited in recent times. Scarcity of water and serious congestion at the many locks in the upper part of the canal forced the ironmasters to bypass this section in 1802 by building the Penydarren Tramroad from Merthyr to Abercynon. Along this tramroad, Richard Trevithick's steam locomotive pulled a train of trams from Penydarren Ironworks to the canal at Abercynon in 1804.

The head offices of the canal company were in a nearby building which is now the Navigation Hotel. The Superintendent or Manager for several late Victorian decades was Thomas Shepherd JP. Administration of the canal was difficult in its earlier years without telephone or penny post, and a horseman often galloped off with urgent messages. Toll-collectors, security bonded for their honesty, were positioned along the canal. They examined boat permits, checked the weights of boats and received the tolls or charges due. After the passing of the Constables Act in 1840 the canal company employed its own police and Thomas Thomas acted as their constable in Pontypridd in 1898.

The Aberdare Canal, opened in 1812, joined the Glamorganshire Canal behind Lock Street at Abercynon. For most of the Victorian years the canal between Abercynon and Pontypridd passed through open fields until, from 1886, the villages of Cilfynydd, Pontshonnorton, Coedpenmaen, and Trallwn Gardens sprang up after the sinking of the Albion Colliery at Cilfynydd in 1884. This whole stretch of the canal ran through the meadows of Ynysydwr across from Parc Newydd farm and ran alongside the Navigation Road over the Cilfynydd or Craig Evan Leyshon Common. Along this quiet reach, a boatman could enjoy

the summer charms of the canal edged with cornfields riddled with
scarlet poppies and blue cornflowers as the boat floated towards the
Cilfynydd Inn set away in the distance below Coed Pant-du. The canal
entered Cilfynydd at Lock Cottage where a lock stepped it down to
pass beneath a small humpbacked bridge which gave access from
Cilfynydd Road to the Albion Colliery and the playing fields beyond.
The colliery sprawled over John Rosser's farm which bore Cilfynydd's
earlier name of Ynyscaedudwg.

Canal horses were usually stabled near a lock or at wharves owned
by the canal company or by private carriers. Boats also moored at night
at canalside inns with stables, since the journey from Merthyr to
Cardiff could take more than 24 hours. At Cilfynydd horses were
stabled in what became later the Cwm Cottages where Cilfynydd
Rugby Football Club social club is now sited. The canal curved away
from the Cilfynydd Inn and the few cottages which in the 1860s made
up the hamlet. The stretch to Quarry Siding had a towpath bordering
'Yr Waun', a copse that faced the majestic Graig-yr-Hesg mountain and
tumbled down to the banks of a River Taff filled with salmon and trout.
On the village side of the canal a backdrop featured the birch-clad
slopes of Coed Bodwenarth (or Bedwenarth) and the hills that reached
to the heights of Eglwysilan mountain. At Quarry Siding many canal
horses were shod at the farriers and blacksmith's shop on a site later
occupied by King's Garage. Boats were loaded near here with stone
from the depot belonging to Bodwenarth Quarries.

Many villagers would not dare pass this spot unescorted for fear of
seeing the ghost that reputedly walked the short length of Police Row.
One determined ghostbuster, a stalwart miner with a pick handle at the
ready, prowled for months along the road until one solemn twilight
when he saw the phantom figure by the site of an old toll-house, and
fled full pelt to the Bassett Hotel and the Royal Oak to fortify himself
with whisky before the journey home.

There were nearly 200 boats on the canal in 1830, some owned by
the canal company and others by local carriers. The tolls paid by the
carriers were calculated on their written declarations of the cargo,
endorsed by the toll-collector. He could check the tonnage by gauging:
the depth at which every new boat floated when empty and when
carrying various tonnages was determined and figures marked at several
levels on the boat with notches or iron plates. Later, the figures were
recorded in toll books. At Tongwynlais Lock the canal company

erected a weighing machine which simplified checks for overweight cargo. For many years the tolls were 1d and then 2d per ton per mile for coal, iron, stone, brick, tile, sand, gravel and manure, until the coming of the railways weakened the canal's finances.

The canal reached the stone bridge at Pontshonnorton (Pontsion-norton, or John Norton's bridge) where boats loaded the coal mined in the small Bodwenarth Colliery sunk in the early 1870s by William Williams of Penygraig. His partner, William Morgan, built and lived at Bronwydd House in Tyfica Road and also built St Catherine's Church in 1868 for which John Norton was the architect. The colliery, approached originally by a 10ft wide wooden bridge over the canal, was abandoned in the early 1880s.

The canal ran past Belgrave Terrace and the Swamp to the bridge at the foot of Coronation Terrace by Parsons bakery. The bridge was known as 'The Distillery Bridge' because it gave access to the nearby Chivers distillery and chemical works, which despatched much of its production by boat. The canal then ran parallel to Coedpenmaen Road to a lock opposite Baptist Chapel, overlooked by the hillside of Ty Gwyn where the Pontypridd Golf Club was founded in 1905.

Boatmen were also a fruitful source of news and gossip. They talked of victories and defeats in the Empire or the progress of troops called out during coalfield disputes in South Wales. They considered the sad news of the Great Western Colliery disasters of August 1892 and April 1893, when 121 lives were lost, or recoiled on that grey Saturday afternoon of 23 June 1894 when word spread that an explosion at the Albion Colliery in Cilfynydd had killed 290 miners.

The canal reached a bridge and lock across from the Newbridge Arms of 1735 and flowed into a small basin beside an overflow weir and boat building yard in front of Foundry Place before descending through double locks, connecting with the short length of private canal to Hopkin Morgan's East Street bakery and reaching the wharf by the Queens Hotel. Here was the canal stores of William R. Davies. He and his son John carried cargoes daily between Pontypridd and Cardiff. On the other side of the canal was a high building called the Corn Stores. It was established in 1850 by William Lewis and traded for nearly a century. Supplies were winched up from the canal boats and corn was ground by steam-powered machinery. The whole area, including a lock and a bridge, was cleared in the 1970s for the A470 trunk road and is now dominated by a flyover and roundabout.

The Queens Hotel lock was a favourite place for spectators to watch the boats going through the lock and unloading supplies for the town. Boatmen were besieged for their stories about the Relief of Mafeking in mid-May 1900 when British troops were relieved after holding out against a superior number of Boers for seven months. The troops included men of the 3rd Volunteer Battalion of the Welsh Regiment whose headquarters were in Ceridwen Terrace opposite the Maltsters Arms by the Old Bridge. Boats tied up along the wharf on the Friday night and their crews joined in the rejoicing and celebrating by the singing, flag-waving crowds who squeezed into the local pubs until the bars ran dry.

On the Saturday, the boatmen garlanded their craft with towels for the lack of flags and had the day off as did all the local colliers, chainmakers and most other workers to enjoy a celebration gala in a field lent by Lewis Gordon Lenox JP at nearby Ynysangharad. J.P. Charles, an agent for the Cotton Powder Co., set off explosives in the field and on Coed Craig-yr-Hesg and the salvos, which could be heard in Llantwit Fardre, caused a lone horse to bolt into the canal with its startled boy attendant who nearly drowned before being rescued.

On Sunday morning, the boats soberly set off again on the canal which curved past Canal Place—opposite Park View—from where Thomas Thomas and Mrs Martha Thomas carried goods daily to Cardiff for several decades. The canal continued alongside Ynys-angharad Road and the Newbridge Chainworks of Brown Lenox where barges unloaded iron and coal supplies. Here, about 80 yards above the upper gates of a pair of locks (Nos 31 and 32), water entered a top basin off the canal and was channelled to drive water-wheels that worked some chain-making machinery before flowing away under the chainworks proving room and test house to a large bottom basin. Wrought iron chain cable and anchors forged by the highly skilled smiths employed by Brown Lenox were lowered through the floor of the test house into a barge waiting below.

In 1824 nearly a thousand tons of Brown Lenox iron products were carried on the canal. In 1835 their shipments had increased to 2,500 tons and in 1839 reached 4,000 tons. In 1803 boats carried a total of 10,000 tons of iron on the canal. In 1820 the figure had risen to nearly 50,000 tons in addition to 38,000 tons of coal. By 1830 shipments increased to 82,000 tons of iron and 114,000 tons of coal, of which 46,000 tons came from the Dinas pits of Walter Coffin. He was replaced as the leading shipper on the canal in the 1830s by Thomas Powell whose operations led to the formation of the Powell Duffryn Co. In 1840 Thomas Powell shipped 62,000 tons of coal, about a quarter of the total on the canal, from his collieries at Gelligaer and Aberdare. That year, iron shipments totalled 132,000 tons. Despite the building of the Taff Vale Railway, 1851 saw canal shipments of 287,000 tons of iron and 294,000 tons of coal.

Beer, ales and stout were consigned locally from the Ynysangharad Brewery and Bottling Stores of the still busy Bunch of Grapes Inn near the chainworks bridge. Some boatmen with valuable cargoes of tobacco, wines, spirits, tea, sugar and other goods yielded to a temptation to steal. A dishonest boatman used a small pump to draw off some spirit from a cask in which he had drilled a hole under the iron hoop. Water was sometimes pumped into the cask to conceal the loss before the hole was sealed and the hoop replaced. Publicans suspicious of a particular person found it difficult to prove the theft.

Part of the bottom basin by the chainworks bridge, a lockkeeper's cottage and a stretch of canal through the picturesque Nightingale's Bush were restored by the Glamorgan Naturalists' Trust and opened in 1979 by the Prince of Wales. This nature reserve has been cleaned again recently by the Pontypridd branch of the Glamorgan Wildlife Trust and Pontypridd Town Council plans further restoration work.

Stone from John Gibbon's quarry behind the Farmers Arms was sent by canal at this point. The canal passed under the 1884 viaduct of the Pontypridd, Caerphilly & Newport Railway. Rails made at the Taff Vale Ironworks just over the River Taff at Treforest were sent by trams across the 1851 iron bridge for loading on to barges. Close by on the Pentrebach Road was the Duke of Bridgewater Arms, the 'Old Duke', where in earlier years teams of horses could be changed for the stage coaches running from Merthyr to Cardiff. The inn was converted into a private house by Lady Llanover and called Yr Hen Dy, 'the old house'. Lady Llanover was Augusta Waddington, the heiress of Llanover, who married Sir Benjamin Hall, later Lord Llanover, who became a principal landowner in Pontypridd and whose mother was Charlotte, a daughter of William Crawshay I.

Here in Glyntaff the canal was overlooked by the Round Houses which Dr William Price erected in 1859 at Graig-yr-Helfa as a lodge for a mansion that was never built. He held his surgery in a house nearby. The canal passed below St Mary's Church, built in 1839, and

Mrs Ann Aldworth's Charity Schools of the 1860s near a turnpike gate to reach the humpbacked bridge by the Llanbradach Arms. It ran in front of the old Gwern-y-Gerwn houses and on past the west side of the gasworks of 1897. Here, for a short distance, it ran close to the Doctor's Canal until the two canals made their different ways to connect later at Dynea.

Doctor's Canal

The Doctor's Canal was cut by Dr Richard Griffiths, who was born in 1756 at Gellifendigaid, near Glyncoch, in the parish of Llanwonno. In 1790 he opened a coal level at Gyfeillon, near Trehafod, and in 1808 leased the coal under the Hafod and Llandraw farms belonging to his brother-in-law, Evan Morgan. He granted sub-leases in 1809 to Sir Jeremiah Homfray and others and built a three-mile-long tramroad from Gyfeillon to convey the coal to the Glamorganshire Canal at Treforest. A year later the tramroad linked up with another built by Walter Coffin, which ran from Dinas, further up the valley. The Doctor's tramroad ran along the west bank of the Rhondda, through Hopkinstown, along Sardis Road to the Tumble in Pontypridd and down the Tramroad or Broadway to the weighing machine at Taff House, Treforest.

The weighing machine was still standing in 1902 and apparently colliers were paid according to the amounts of coal weighed on it. Dr Griffiths built the three-arch stone Machine Bridge, called 'Pont-y-Doctor', over the Taff, which was completed in 1809. The tramroad crossed the bridge and ran down to Castle Inn Bridge (widened in 1887 from 13ft to 26ft) and to the weir by the Gwern-y-Gerwn turnpike gate on the Cardiff Road. From a point behind the present engineering company's premises, once the site of a Victorian hide and wool market and later a slaughterhouse, Dr Griffiths constructed a mile-long private canal. It ran parallel to and above the old Cardiff Road to a small bridge near the Maltsters Arms on the west side of Ebenezer Street in Rhydyfelin. Further down, a tramroad from the Treforest Tinplate Works crossed Julia Bridge over the Taff to meet the canal, which continued along the present Poplar Road to the dock at Dynea where it joined the Glamorganshire Canal in 1813. A century later the urban district council filled the Doctor's Canal with ashes when it was intended to run an extension of the town's electric tramways over it.

Above: Two locks, footbridge, and lower basin of the Glamorganshire Canal alongside Brown Lenox Chainworks. A lock-keeper's cottage remains to the right near the Bunch of Grapes Hotel in Ynysangharad Road. **Below:** The canal at Glyntaff. The iron tramroad bridge over the Taff serving the Taff Vale Ironworks crossed here. The Duke of Bridgewater Arms on the left is demolished. In the distance is St Mary's, also the gasworks.

Above: The lock and lock-keeper's cottage at Dynea (originally Denia) at the end of Poplar Road. Cardinal Newman School playing fields are above the slope. Rhydyfelin Non-Political Club is sited at Blaen-y-Llyn in the background to the left. **Below:** Lock Lewis on the canal at Rhydyfelin in the 1920s.

Above: Canal bridge and Queens Hotel lock at Corn Stores Hill, *c.* 1899. **Below:** Canal bridge at Glyntaff, near the old Llanbradach Arms, *c.* 1899.

Above: River Rhondda meets the River Taff. This Victorian view shows the River Rhondda bridge joining Pontypridd High Street to Taff Street, Brunel's skew bridge beyond, and the expanse of Ynysangharad Fields, now the Park. **Below:** View of Trallwn, *c.* 1950, showing the White Bridge lower centre.

Above: View of Trallwn, 1957, showing Merthyr Road on left and the Glamorganshire Canal towpath centre right. The building in lower centre is the Royal Oak Hotel. The canal route is now the A470. **Below:** The River Taff with three of its bridges in the 1950s, also the old gasometer in Gas Lane. Today's main post office on the Tumble is bottom left and the old slaughterhouse is bottom right.

Above: The reinforced concrete White Bridge over the River Taff at the top of Berw Road, 1938. The bridge was opened in 1909. It was reported in May 1899 that a Trallwn Iron Bridge was opened at or near the site although there is no known photographic evidence. **Below:** View of the River Taff, showing the three-arch Machine Bridge built in 1809, St Mary's Church, the Round Houses and the old turnpike road, originally a tramroad to the Doctor's Canal near the weir by Castle Inn Bridge, Treforest. The pointed tip to the tower of St Mary's has long disappeared.

Above: Aqueduct at the Berw, carrying a private water supply from the Clydach at Glyncoch and then down Feeder Row (the older part of West Street) to Brown Lenox Chainworks. **Below:** Canal bridge by the Queens Hotel, *c.* 1899.

Above: View of Glyntaff in the 1940s, showing St Mary's Church and Mrs Aldworth's Charity Schools of Victorian times. The bridge crosses the Glamorganshire Canal by the old Llanbradach Arms which was set back just to the left of foreground. **Below:** The Berw Pool looking towards Cilfynydd, *c.* 1900.

Above: The Old Bridge and the Victoria Bridge in the 1950s. **Below:** The single-span Old Bridge, completed in 1756. Alongside and downstream is the Victoria Bridge built in 1857 and widened in 1897. Sion Street is on the left. Photograph 1899.

Above: Cilfynydd Road, looking towards Police Row, Pontshonnorton, showing 'missing' stone and wooden cottages (Nos 1–4), *c.* 1900. **Below:** Baptist Chapel, Coedpenmaen, with the canal on the banking to the left, *c.* 1900.

Griffiths shipped 6,000 tons of coal on his canal in 1820 and Walter Coffin shipped 10,500 tons. Griffiths was one of eight children of William and Elizabeth Griffiths who owned much land and property at Glyncoch, Gelliwion, and in the Gelliwastad and Tyfica areas of Pontypridd. He practised medicine in Cardiff and became a justice of the peace. His sister Jane married Thomas Thomas of Llanbradach and one of their descendants was Clara Thomas of Llwynmadoc (Breconshire), the heiress to the Griffiths property and fortune, who was a distinguished and benevolent citizen of Victorian Pontypridd. Dr Griffiths died in 1826 and was buried in the churchyard at Llanwonno.

Glamorganshire Canal

Meanwhile, the Glamorganshire Canal continued along what is now Ilan Avenue to reach the picturesque Lock Lewis at Gellidawel, Rhydyfelin. Prior to its growth in Victorian times, the hamlet of Rhydyfelin was the home of several families with the surname of John—after two brothers of that name gave up working on farms at Eglwysilan and became boatmen on the canal in 1794.

Lock Lewis is possibly named after its first lock-keeper who lived in a nearby cottage. Mrs Mary Powell lived there for 50 years until 1972 and made many shopping trips by canal boat. Her husband, John Powell, was a Pontypridd UDC transport manager and his father Morgan Powell was a lock-keeper at Lock Lewis. Boats used on the canal were usually 60ft long by 8ft wide and carried 20–24 tons of cargo. They had a crew of two: one led the horse on the towpath while the other steered the boat by a wooden tiller, which fitted into the large rudder. A steam-powered boat was used on the Pontypridd to Cardiff section of the canal in 1890 but its speed created too much wash and steam boats were not used generally until 1911.

After passing under the Dyffryn Road bridge at Rhydyfelin, the canal ran behind the length of today's Sycamore Street, the playing fields of Heol-y-Celyn school and Cardinal Newman Roman Catholic school to reach the wide basin at Dynea, where it was joined by the Doctor's Canal at Blaen-y-Llyn on which the Rhydyfelin Non-Political Club is now situated. Gorvett's boat-repairing dock was here and the walls of Dynea Lock and the lock-keeper's cottage by a little hump-backed bridge could be seen during recent excavations for flood prevention measures.

In Victorian times Dynea was spelt Denia ('attractive location') and the area was a favourite spot for picnics and rambles. Up to a hundred people would sit on cross-planks on a boat destined for Dynea to enjoy the views and walks over the wooded hillsides below Mynydd Eglwysilan and Mynydd Mayo. Sunday Schools from Pontypridd and Cardiff hired boats and met at Dynea to join in organised games and community hymn-singing in the fields near the lock.

The canal was frozen over for six weeks in 1895 and many people enjoyed skating fiestas at Dynea. Thick winter frosts and ice often stopped movement on the canal and, before the coming of the railways, many collieries were unable to despatch their output. Fog was another hazard, as was ice that could cut into the wooden hull of a boat. Iron-built ice-boats, rocked by lines of men aboard and hauled by teams of horses on the slippery towpath, were used to keep the canal open during hard winters.

Just along from Dynea Lock an eighty-yard stretch of the canal was breached in 1908, when tree trunks felled on the hillsides above Dan-yr-Allt were carried down the slopes by heavy October rains and blocked the sluice-gates of the lock. As the water could not be released from the canal, pressure built up and the towpath collapsed down a steep embankment. Traffic was held up for several weeks and cargoes were off-loaded on to carts which shuttled to and from the breached area.

From Dynea, the canal ran through the fields of Gellihirion Farm (where the Tesco Superstore is now sited) overlooked by Cwrt-y-Celyn Farm and the woodlands of Forestnewydd below Mynydd Mayo. On a hot summer day a boatman could welcome a drink of cider from a stone jar offered by the Gellihirion haymakers as they pitchforked the long windrows of harvest on to the great, creaking haywains. He could bargain with local farmers for supplies of eggs, bacon and cheese, or with anglers for part of their catch—often with part of his cargo.

A boatman in late Victorian years earned about 35s for a 48-hour week when in regular employment but when he was held up by ice or drought—such as the severe drought in the the summer of 1899—his wages could be halved. Many boatmen found it increasingly difficult to make a living, particularly after competition from the Taff Vale Railway forced cuts in canal tolls and, subsequently, in wage rates.

The canal passed close to the Upper Boat Inn and hugged the

meadows where the Treforest Industrial Estate was built in the 1930s. A half-mile length of tramroad linked Brockett Grover's Maesmawr Colliery to the canal. At Nantgarw, boats took on barrels and boxes of china or earthenware from the china works before moving on to negotiate the treble locks at Taffs Well and then on to Tongwynlais.

When the canal company decided to simplify checking the weights of cargoes, Brown Lenox chainworks designed and constructed a weighing machine consisting of a cast iron framework measuring 32ft long by 12½ft wide with an overhead system of levers from which a 45ft long cradle was suspended. The framework was placed over the Tongwynlais Lock in 1834. After a barge was floated into the lock, the gates were closed. When the sluice gates opposite were opened the water drained away and the barge settled into the cradle and its weight was recorded. The weighbridge could weigh accurately up to 40 tons. In 1850 it was moved to the Crockherbtown Lock near the entrance to the canal tunnel and in 1894 it was placed at the North Road Lock in Cardiff.

The Merthyr to Abercynon section of the canal did not survive the whole of Queen Victoria's reign: it bowed to railway competition and closed in 1898. The section between Abercynon and Cilfynydd closed in 1915 and the remaining section between there and Cardiff followed in 1942. The whole canal was officially abandoned in January 1944.

Rivers and Bridges

Canals, rivers and bridges played an important role in the development of Pontypridd. The Taff and the Rhondda, which flow through the town centre, supplied water and a source of power in Victorian times for corn mills, cloth mills, tanneries, a brewery, ironworks, chainworks, tinplate works and other industries.

The Taff rises in two heads in the Brecon Beacons, known as the Taff Fawr and the Taff Fechan, which join at Cyfarthfa, where they fed the Glamorganshire Canal. Flowing southwards, the Taff is joined by the Bargoed Taff at Quakers Yard, continues to a junction with the Cynon at Abercynon and meanders to meet the Clydach at Glyncoch Mill. From its confluence with the Clydach the Taff winds through the meadows of Cilfynydd to the Berw below Coed Craig-yr-Hesg just north of Pontypridd. The blasting of rocks in the river bed at Graig-yr-

Hesg destroyed the once wild beauty of the Berw Pool with its salmon leap and pretty cascade.

The Berw Pool was a popular spot for picnickers but very dangerous for swimmers and the *Pontypridd Observer* frequently reported the drowning of young bathers. A viaduct was erected over the river just here in 1885 to carry the Taff Vale mineral line to the Albion Colliery at Cilfynydd and, later, passenger trains between Pontypridd and Nelson. The disused line (but not the viaduct) now forms part of the Taff Heritage Trail. By the viaduct can still be seen the debris of stone buttresses which supported an aqueduct that carried a private water supply to Brown Lenox chainworks from the Clydach at Glyncoch and through West Street, or Feeder Row.

In August 1898 Pontypridd Urban District Council approved a provisional order to build an iron road bridge over the Taff at the Berw to relieve the severe congestion of carts and carriages using the canal bridge by the Queens Hotel on the road to Cilfynydd. It was reported in May 1899 that the Trallwn Iron Bridge would be ready in two weeks. There seems to be no other report or photographic evidence of the bridge. The present reinforced concrete White Bridge at the Berw was opened on 6 April 1909. The Berw riverside was attractively lined with trees in 1899 and a small park laid out in front of Lewis Terrace. The area was completed in June 1900 and named Victoria Recreation Grounds. Nearby was a well called Ffynnon Gellidawel which supposedly could cure eye ailments and even restore sight.

Downstream is the famous Old Bridge from which Pontypridd takes its name. The single-span structure was depicted by artists and writers as 'a rainbow from the lightness, width and elevation of the arch, the beau ideal of architectural elegance, rising from the steep bank on one side of a salmon river and resting gracefully on the other side and situated between the beauty of steep, wooded hillsides'.

The name of Pontypridd has known various spellings: one of the oldest was Pont-yr-Hen-dy-Pridd, 'the bridge of the old earthen house', and reputedly so called because of a lodge of earth and stone erected near the site by the workmen. It was also Pont-y-ty-Pridd which was shortened to Pontypridd, a spelling used by several writers before 1789. The town was also known as Newbridge until 1856.

The bridge was built by William Edwards who was born on 8 February 1719, the youngest son of a farmer at Ty Canol Farm on Eglwysilan mountain. As a young man Edwards was keenly interested in working with dry stone. He became expert at repairing and building walls for neighbouring farmers and learned his craft by building several houses, forges and mills in the parish of Eglwysilan. He apparently took much interest in the great walls of nearby Caerphilly Castle. Local farmers despaired at being unable to cross the River Taff at Pontypridd except when the water level was low enough to use a ford opposite today's health centre by the park gates and commissioned the young mason to build a bridge for £500.

His first bridge was a three-arch structure built in 1746 and sited slightly downstream of the present bridge. It was short-lived: after 2½ years, while Edwards watched anxiously, tree trunks and other debris battered the bridge during a severe flood and the bridge, not having sufficient height and strength to withstand the onslaught, collapsed and was washed away. Edwards had undertaken to maintain the bridge for seven years and had to reconstruct it. He conceived the idea of a one-arch bridge, the perfect segment of a circle, 35ft high with a 140ft chord or span, and a diameter of 175ft. Edwards and Pontypridd wheelwright Thomas Williams built a substantial centring or framing to support the arch while it was under construction. Stone for the bridge was quarried locally. But when the bridge was nearing completion in 1751 the centring and arch collapsed.

Edwards was in debt and discouraged, but a subscription of £700 promoted by Lord Talbot and Lord Windsor enabled him to finish the bridge. Edwards did not know the laws of equilibrium, or balance, and the pressure caused by the 32ft long by 20ft high abutments, or haunches, of the bridge was so great that after several years the crown of the arch was forced upwards and the central section collapsed. Undaunted, Edwards lightened the weight of the haunches by making three cylindrical openings (3ft, 6ft and 9ft in diameter) in each. The danger that the light curve of the bridge would spring upwards again was avoided. The Old Bridge was completed in 1756 and was for many years one of the longest single-span bridges standing in the world.

William Edwards also built bridges at Aberavon, Llandovery, Morriston, Usk and Glastonbury. His son David built Newport Bridge and others at Bedwas and Llandeilo. William Edwards lived for many years at Bryn Tail Farm high above Glyntaff. After being converted by the famous revivalist Howell Harries in 1739 he became a lay preacher and while building the bridge at Morriston he also built a chapel there and presented it to the congregation. He was ordained as a Welsh

Independent Minister at Groeswen Congregational Chapel and gave his salary to the poor. He held the post until his death on 7 August 1789 and was buried just outside the south door of Eglwysilan church.

The Old Bridge proved too steep for heavy farm waggons which had to be dragged up one side with strong chains or ropes and extra horses. A large block was often attached to the back of the cart by a long rope and as the cart descended the other side of the bridge the block was pulled up the steep ascent and acted as a brake. Frequently, horses fell and carts careered out of control. Travellers either risked injury or alighted from their carriages and crossed the bridge on foot.

During the early Victorian years the coming of the Taff Vale Railway, the growth of local industry and the opening of many steam-coal pits in the Rhondda and other areas increased the importance of Pontypridd. The Old Bridge could not cope with the streams of carts and carriages which barely had room to pass each other and so it was planned to build another bridge beside it. Many Pontypriddians resented the proposals for siting the new bridge so close to the old as to destroy the graceful attraction of a 'wonder of the world of Wales'.

Most traffic still used the river ford and applications were made by the local solicitor Edward Colnett Spickett for the new bridge to be built by Glamorgan Quarter Sessions. All hope of this was eventually abandoned and several prominent Pontypridd citizens, including the postmaster Charles Bassett, formed a committee to raise a public subscription. Meetings were held at the Tredegar Arms throughout 1853 and, to aid publicity, a hot-air balloon was launched from a field adjacent to the gasworks alongside the river. Crowds watched the ascent of the balloon which came down near Caerphilly Castle. Dr William Price held a tea party at the Rocking Stone on the Common to boost the fund. The increasing traffic through the town resorted more and more to using the ford and the urgency for providing a new bridge was evidenced in June 1854 when a pair of horses and a phaeton carriage were swept away. A tragedy was avoided only by a brave rescue by employees of the nearby gasworks.

The bridge committee chose Robert Hughes as architect and his design for a three-arch structure so impressed the Revd G. Thomas of Ystrad Mynach and the management of Brown Lenox chainworks that each donated £500. The bridge cost £1,575. Building stone was obtained from the Trallwn Quarry owned by Morgan Edwards. In the centre of the bridge (then 20ft wide) a stone was inscribed: 'This bridge was erected in A.D. 1857 by public subscription. Designed by Robert Hughes and built by Thomas Jenkins'.

Before the opening ceremony in December 1857, the Pontypridd Drum and Fife Band and the Treforest Brass Band marched through the town playing *See the Conquering Hero Comes* and other tunes. Commanded by Police Superintendent James Thomas, a large procession of carriages, horsemen and marchers escorted by constables filed over the bridge to meet the Revd Thomas on Merthyr Road and escort him over the bridge. Banners at the ends of the bridge proclaimed 'Patience Rewarded' and 'Unity is Strength'. The bridge was dedicated to public service at a colourful ceremony in nearby Tabernacle Square at which an official photograph was taken by Taliesin Williams, son of the poet Gwilym Morganwg. There followed a grand lunch and speeches to celebrate the opening of the new bridge and the belated centenary of the Old Bridge.

Some years later the river below the bridge was weired to prevent scouring of the foundations, and dashing young Victorians in punts and rowing boats were a familiar sight on the small lake and upstream stretch of the river to the Berw. When new iron-girder parapets were placed across the widened (34ft) bridge in September 1897 the urban district council decided to name the bridge the Victoria Bridge in celebration of the Queen's Diamond Jubilee the previous June. Two huge incandescent gaslamps brightly illuminated the bridge throughout the winter nights that followed. In June 1898 the council built a grand iron staircase down to the river bank between the Victoria Bridge and the Maltsters Arms, which was to lead to a boat-stage, but the repairs needed to the weir in 1899 were never carried out and the weir stonework and the ideas for a mooring place were washed away.

At the southern end of a strip of land (once known as 'the sands') in Ynysangharad Park, a footbridge was built across the River Taff in the summer of 1897. It was proposed originally to build it opposite the Arcade from Market Square. A later (1923) concrete bridge at the chosen spot was weakened by recent storms and it was demolished and replaced by a cable-stay bridge in October 1991. Nearby, a two-arch stone bridge over the River Rhondda carries Taff Street past the front of Marks & Spencer and other shops. A narrow wooden bridge crossed here before 1792.

Just below the bridge the Rhondda joins the Taff which then winds around Ynysangharad and flows on to Cardiff and the sea.

Chapter 3

Railway Lines

Excitement bubbled over when shouts of 'Here it is!' rippled along the crowded platform and heralded the approach of the smoke-wreathed engine and its trail of carriages to Pontypridd's St David's station high up on the hill. The train squealed to a stop in a hiss of steam. Doors were hurriedly opened and the day trippers scrambled aboard in a sea of buckets and spades, bags, baskets, babies, bowler hats, caps, plaited straw-boaters and bonnets.

Children clustered round the compartment windows to wave goodbye to the Graig station staff. The stationmaster looked intently at his large watch and blew hard on his whistle as the second hand signalled the start of the outing to the magic of Barry Island. A farewell piping whistle echoed through the village and the engine huffed and puffed as it flexed its muscles of steel. Its rods and wheels gathered strength and the train surged into the tunnel at the end of the platform. Many frantic attempts to strap up the windows were too late and smoke and steam swirled in on the passengers in the unlit carriages.

Bright sunshine greeted the train once more when it emerged from the tunnel and steamed into the Barry Railway station above the Llantwit Road at Treforest. The platform pulsed with activity as mothers and fathers or Sunday School teachers shepherded their flocks aboard. A tiny armada of boys in sailor suits added a splash of blue to the drab grey of suits worn by most boys who mixed with girls clad in long dark dresses draped with white pinafores, high-buttoned boots and straw-hats.

The train moved on and tooted its way up to the Devil's Bridge which stepped down the hillside near the Treforest Tinplate Works and also spanned, at a lower level, the Taff Vale Railway line between Pontypridd and Cardiff. Window-watchers urged more speed from the engine-driver to keep pace with the plume of smoke from a train across the wide valley as it left Dynea for Caerphilly and Newport. But the Barry Island train chugged contentedly along the short stretch of line to Tonteg and then headed into the Vale, rattling through Efail Isaf,

Creigiau and St Fagans. It raced along embankments which harvested views of fields in green and brown and gold, patchworked between neat hedgerows and stately deciduous woodlands. Telegraph poles retreated more hurriedly along the track as the engine saluted signal-boxes and squeezed into cuttings to shroud road bridges in steam and smoke. Passing mineral trains wreaked a havoc of noise and brought shocks of inrushing air and the smell and taste of sulphur. Carriages swayed to the clacking rhythms of speeding wheels and echoed the engine's sharp whistle of warning as the train entered the long tunnel beyond St Fagans. Window-straps were again pulled up with urgency but, inevitably, there erupted the anguished choruses of 'Mam, I've got something in my eye!' Mothers, well schooled in the art, brought succour with the corner of a handkerchief. Oh, the relief when that painful speck of grit was wiped away!

The train hastened on to rapturous claims of 'I can see the sea!' The train curved through ancient Cadoxton and the new Barry Docks until signals brought it to a stop amid the endless domino clanking of couplings from goods wagons shunting alongside—many wagons filled with coal hewn from pits in the valleys. An array of dockside cranes and coal-hoists loaded up the hungry steam-powered freighters and a forest of tall-masted sailing ships soon to catch the trade winds to the world's ports.

Joyously, the train arrived at Barry Island station and the engine lay enveloped in a proud steam of perspiration as the trippers headed across the sand dunes to the beach. Children tucked into their free packets of buns and Welshcakes and bottles of milk. Adventurous paddlers thrilled to the surges of the sea between their toes and dodged being splashed by bathers who streaked from the rows of bathing machines or sentry-box changing rooms to dive into the sparkling waters of Whitmore Bay, often experienced by the mouthful. Sunlit seas and sand-castles contrasted brightly with the more familiar blackened rain-puddles and spoil-tips of home. Babbling voices and laughter mingled with the querulous cries of seagulls and the jingling harness of donkeys giving beach rides.

Many families enjoyed a bracing walk up past Friars Point House, built by ironmaster Francis Crawshay in 1858, and then out along the headland with its views of Cold Knap. Men clad in Sunday-best suits escorted women elegantly dressed in fashionable long skirts, blouses, ties and ribboned straw-hats, and shaded by delicate parasols. They joined other strollers around the wooden Treharne Pier which ran from the Point into Whitmore Bay. (The pier, demolished in 1902, was also built by Crawshay in 1858.) On the other side of the bay, beach-combers with treasure-filled imaginations ambled beside the seashore, or explored the rock pools at Nell's Point before they sauntered up the grassy slopes (later the site of Butlin's holiday camp) that basked beneath blue skies flecked with gaily coloured kites.

There was lunch to enjoy at the seaside refreshment rooms before cockles and sweets and bottles of pop from the few trade stalls near the packed beach. More games to be played in the wide dunes—once a rabbit warren from which a local farmer made a good profit. There were boats trips round the bay and shells to collect as the hours flew by before it was back to the refreshment rooms for tea.

By the time the trippers straggled back to the station their appetites were satisfied and their energies were spent. The congregation on the platform welcomed the return of the train. They sprawled in the carriages and brushed sand from their boots and shoes and stockings and ears and noses and hair. Everywhere. Damp, sand-caked towels were pressed with relief against sunburnt faces. Mothers were thankful that the day had been fine: memories of rainswept hours spent dragging a soaked and bedraggled family around an unsheltered Barry Island were painful. This day fulfilled its promise of a happy break from harsh routine. But the day was done and the train went home to the grey terraces that linked the green hills of Pontypridd.

Taff Vale Railway

The development of Pontypridd as a railway town was due primarily to the coming of the Taff Vale Railway (TVR). Great difficulties were experienced in carrying the growing output from the ironworks and coal mines in the valleys converging on Pontypridd to Cardiff. The Glamorganshire Canal was congested almost from its opening in 1794 and in 1799 the ironmasters promoted a bill in Parliament for a railway to run from the Cardiff Sea Lock up to Abercynon, from where a branch would run to Aberdare, while the main line would continue to Rhymney, with a branch to the limestone quarries beyond Merthyr. The bill was withdrawn after considerable opposition from the canal company.

Above: A Victorian view of Pontypridd from the Graig, showing on left the seven-arch railway viaduct to the Rhondda Valley; St Catherine's Church, centre; River Taff, Old Bridge and Victoria Bridge centre right. **Below:** An early Edwardian view of Cilfynydd. Opposite the Commercial Hotel and below the now demolished Workmen's Hall is seen part of the four-span, 360ft long Coronation Bridge erected in 1902 over the Glamorganshire Canal and Albion Colliery sidings to serve passengers using the Cilfynydd TVR station, closed in 1932.

Above: Taff Vale Railway delivery cart in Market Street. The alleyway takes a flight of narrow steps down into Taff Street. **Below:** Cardiff Road, Rhydyfelin, in 1910.

Above: Children waiting for an excursion train to arrive at the Treforest Taff Vale Station which was opened in 1847. **Below:** Berw railway viaduct, 1899, which still stands. Built in 1885 to carry the TVR mineral line to the Albion Colliery at Cilfynydd and, from 1900, passenger trains between Pontypridd and Nelson.

Above: The seven-arch rail viaduct at Mill Street in 1991. **Below:** Brunel's skew stone-arch bridge and the widened section, looking down Mill Street towards the town, also photographed in 1991.

Above: Canal Place, Queens Hotel, Crown Inn, Llanover Arms, *c.* 1899. **Below:** High Street, railway bridge to the Graig, *c.* 1899.

Until 1830 collieries mainly supplied coking coal to the ironworks and exported any surplus tonnage. But as the population of Glamorgan increased from 71,000 in 1801 to 171,000 in 1841, coal was in demand for brickworks, blacksmiths and the grates of newly built houses. The coal-bearing valleys around Pontypridd were opened up and congestion on the canal increased. Ironmasters again pursued their interest in a railway. In 1835 Isambard Kingdom Brunel estimated the cost of a railway from Cardiff to Merthyr at £190,000 and coalowners and ironmasters held a meeting chaired by Merthyr MP Josiah John Guest to launch a company. Despite renewed opposition from the canal, the Taff Vale Railway Company Act received royal assent on 21 June 1836 and the first commercially important public railway in Wales was incorporated.

The railway would have branches to link with tramroads leading to ironworks at Merthyr and Dowlais and to pits at Nelson, Llancaiach and Dinas Rhondda. Pontypridd would give the long trains of coal a new bridge to the sea at the Bute Dock in Cardiff, opened in 1839. Passenger fares were not to exceed 1½d a mile and company profits were limited originally to 7 per cent. A maximum speed of 12 mph on the main line and branches was fixed by the original Act but restrictions on both profits and speeds were repealed by the Taff Vale Amendment Act of 1840.

Brunel constructed the TVR to the narrow 4ft 8½ins gauge, unlike the broad 7ft gauge of his Great Western Railway. Three factors influenced his decision: the TVR was conceived mainly as a mineral line on which fast speeds were not required, a broad gauge would cause problems in the valleys when extra track was required, and there was a problem concerning curvature of track. Brunel decided against timber bridges for the TVR and built stone viaducts instead, including the 110ft-span skew stone-arch viaduct over the Rhondda in Mill Street which still remains in service, having been widened by the erection of a second stone-arch bridge alongside.

A section of 16 miles from Cardiff to Abercynon was opened on 9 October 1840 and the remainder through to Merthyr on 12 April 1841. The line was single track with passing places only at intermediate stations until powers were obtained in 1857 to double the track. The original Nelson–Llancaiach line also opened in 1841, diverging from the main line at Stormstown Junction between Glyncoch and Abercynon, and a branch built to Dinas. Other than a mineral line extension from Porth to Ynyshir in the Rhondda Fach in 1850, there was no further significant railway penetration of the Rhondda Valleys until 1856. Treforest station opened in 1847.

Initially the TVR had eight engines. There were three classes of passenger coach. The third class were open vans known as tubs with side seats and a centre left free for luggage and animals. Passengers had no shelter from the weather or engine smoke and spent the journey being thrown about the tubs 'in quite lively fashion'. The TVR later introduced covered vans with a door at each end.

The long coal trains found it hazardous to negotiate the sharp curve of the Dinas track into Pontypridd which ran in front of Carmel Baptist Church and behind the cottages at the foot of Graigwen Hill before crossing Brunel's viaduct into the station. Several derailments made a better route necessary and a second viaduct, of seven arches, was built in 1861–2 across the Rhondda opposite Mill Street. In 1872, the Rhondda Cutting, which passed under a bridge by Carmel, gave direct running from the Rhondda to Merthyr.

Pontypridd became an even busier and more important railway junction as coal exploration in the Rhondda Valley increased. Also, 16 steam-coal pits were sunk in the Aberdare valley between 1840 and 1853 and the TVR line from Pontypridd to Aberdare, which branched off at Abercynon (known as Aberdare Junction until 1896) was opened both for passenger and goods trains in August 1846. This created more traffic through Pontypridd. Many passenger trains and nearly 200 goods and empty-wagon trains passed through Pontypridd every day. But on the first Monday of each month in the years 1888 to 1898 the trains were almost exclusively passenger. That day was known as 'Mabon's Day' after Mabon or William Abraham, the Rhondda MP who secured the monthly holiday when every colliery closed and miners and their families packed excursion trains from Pontypridd and the valleys on outings to the seaside.

The TVR backed a plan to convert the old Llantwit Fardre tramroad and connect Llantrisant with the TVR main line at Treforest. Passenger services between Pontypridd and Llantrisant began on 21 January 1875.

Ynysybwl was linked in 1886 by a branch from the Abercynon direction to serve the Lady Windsor Colliery sunk the previous year and passenger trains began in 1890. The Ynysybwl South Curve at Clydach Court opened in 1900 and gave a direct run from Pontypridd, although passenger trains did not operate until 1904. A new Nelson connection was made in 1887 off the main line at Pontshonnorton Junction and crossed the River Taff over the iron viaduct built in 1885 near the Berw Pool. It served the newly productive Albion Colliery at Cilfynydd, and passenger trains started on 1 June 1900 when the line was extended to join the original Nelson line at Ynysydwr Junction above Cilfynydd. To celebrate the new service, streamers and flags decked the engine and ribbons decorated the new TVR coat of arms bearing its dragon. Cheering crowds greeted the train at Coedpenmaen station and fog-signal detonators on the rails marked its approach to Cilfynydd station, alive with colourful bunting and packed with flag-waving villagers. The line continued to Nelson via Travellers Rest where a station opened on 1 May 1901.

Several people were killed in passenger train accidents near Pontypridd. Twelve died and more than 30 were injured in 1878 when two trains collided in the Rhondda Cutting. They were taken to the Graig Workhouse, then the only hospital in Pontypridd. Near the Devil's Bridge on 12 August 1893 several carriages of a train were thrown off the track and hurtled down an embankment facing Upper Boat while the engine stayed on the rails. Rescue gangs covered 13 dead passengers and one rescuer with tarpaulins and laid 60 injured along the grass verges while blankets were hastily acquired.

The original TVR station at Pontypridd in 1840 had one platform and a shed used as a booking office. The TVR horses were stabled in a large building on a site now occupied by Marks & Spencer. To cope with the increasing numbers of trains from the Aberdare valley extra track was laid locally in 1847 and a new two-platform station was built over the old one in Pontypridd. The platforms were lengthened in 1875 and further alterations were completed in 1900 at a cost of £60,000. Extra cattle pens brought more complaints from worshippers who were disturbed on their way to Sunday services by the herds of cattle being driven from the station and under the widened High Street bridge by the Half Moon Hotel to the slaughterhouse on the Broadway. In 1907 the station was reconstructed as one long island platform with three bays for trains which terminated at Pontypridd. It remains so today but is relatively silent compared with its Victorian heyday.

Four new sets of track were laid by the spring of 1897 and a level crossing near the old Ruperra Hotel in Berw Road, which gave access to the new Lanwood schools, became a fearful place for pupils to negotiate. A subway constructed off Morgan Street in April 1898 removed the danger. The nearby goods depot behind Gelliwastad Road was extremely busy from mid-Victorian times. It is now disused and the area is a car park. The former Taff-Ely Borough Council converted the derelict buildings into an indoor bowls centre. In April 1901, another goods station was opened at Cilfynydd to serve the area north of Pontypridd.

The TVR was the only South Wales railway company to build a large number of its own locomotives. Nearly 200 were in service by 1900 when the company resorted more often to purchase and used its workshops for repairs and rebuilding. One of the repair workshops was at the coke ovens in Hopkinstown.

Oscar Hurford became the stationmaster at Pontypridd in October 1899 and was still there during the First World War. John Pennell was a young Victorian ticket collector who remembered clipping shilling return fare tickets to Cardiff and in 1900 saw platforms and trains so crowded that the TVR restricted personal luggage on market days to 60lb. He was a well-known station inspector during the Second World War.

Pontypridd railwaymen knew long hours and low wages. From the early 1870s signalmen earned 20s to 23s for a week averaging 84 hours, often worked in shifts of up to 18 hours. Guards, or brakesmen, worked the same long shifts. On coal trains in the early years, a guard sat on the last wagon and pulled hard on an iron lever on the side of the wagon to brake the speed of the train. Later, a primitive brake-van was attached and a wheel was screwed down to apply brake shoes to the van. When an engine-driver braked, the loose-coupled wagons closed up buffer-to-buffer and if the guard was slow in applying his brake in turn the concertina action would hurl him across the van. A guard named Hurcombe was instantly dismissed merely for grumbling about this 'torture in a dungeon'. The passenger train guard fared better: resplendent in smartly pressed uniform, highly polished boots and with a green flag furled underneath his arm he was the elite of the line. Prompt departure was his responsibility which he enforced with his watch, whistle and iron will.

Many railwaymen earned less than £1 a week for long hours. They included shunters, platelayers, gangers, labourers, examiners, greasers, repairers, cleaners, clerks, porters and ticket collectors. An engine-driver, too, worked long hours—up to 100 a week with shifts of 26 hours if needed. The TVR often fined men a hefty 5s if they left the footplate for even a few minutes to eat their sandwiches. By the late 1890s an engine-driver earned an average of £2 a week.

The Associated Society of Railway Servants (ASRS) was formed in 1871 and ASLEF in 1880. Neither was recognised by the TVR. When the Railway Nine Hours Movement began in 1881 the TVR agreed to reduce working hours but proposed to reduce wages accordingly. A strike to win better wages and conditions by TVR men in the summer of 1900 resulted in a famous law case and far-reaching consequences. The ASRS selected the TVR as a test case to gain recognition of their union. They presented the TVR general manager, Ammon Beasley, with a claim for an increase of 2s a week and double time for Sunday working. The claim was rejected and a total of 800 notices were given in.

On Sunday 19 August hundreds of railwaymen congregated in the Tumble area of Pontypridd for a meeting at the Royal Clarence Theatre. After singing the hymn 'Lead, kindly light' amid the encircling gloom, the men heard the TVR proposals of, generally, an increase of 1s a week. The men rejected the proposals and the strike was on. Next morning, pickets halted early trains to the Rhondda at Porth. Driver Charles Hawkins and fireman Henry Forbear worked a train from Pontypridd to Treherbert without incident but when on their return journey they applied the brake near the coke ovens it could not be released. (No one ever claimed the TVR reward for the arrest of the persons who had tampered with the brake-pipe.) The train rolled to a stop. Pickets swarmed over the engine and the footplate-men were beaten, thrown off the engine and their hands tied. The two men were lashed together and paraded through the streets to the strikers' committee rooms in Pontypridd where they met a tirade of abuse from more angry pickets and were reprimanded by union leaders.

There were no trains the next morning when telegraph wires were cut between Pontypridd and Porth. Local police were reinforced by constables from Bristol and this action angered the strikers who argued that they were justified in their dispute. Two strikers were jailed under the Conspiracy and Property Act. Three men were committed for trial for various offences.

Ammon Beasley secured an interim injunction against the ASRS and the strike collapsed on Friday 31 August when a mass meeting of the men accepted the TVR terms. Early in September the ASRS appealed successfully against the injunction but in the following year the House of Lords reversed the appeal and ruled that it was possible to sue a trade union for damages caused by a trade dispute. The TVR brought an action which was heard before Mr Justice Willis who gave judgment for the company with agreed damages of £23,000. The decision advanced the slow progress of the national Labour Representative Committee which in 1906 adopted the name 'Labour Party'. Years of bitterness at the decision led directly to the Labour Party winning a significant number of seats at the 1906 general election and the subsequent passing of the Trades Dispute Act which remedied the railwaymen's grievance.

Pontypridd, Caerphilly & Newport Railway and Cardiff Railway

The growth of the South Wales coalfield and railway networks led to increasing congestion in Cardiff Docks in the early 1850s. Penarth Dock opened in 1865 and was served by a branch from the TVR main line at Radyr. But both ports became blocked: within twenty years Penarth was shipping three million tons of coal a year and Cardiff over eight million. Apparently, in Cardiff it was possible to walk across the docks on the decks of ships moored side by side awaiting cargo. Coal trains were delayed on their journeys and many collieries were forced to work short time because of a shortage of wagons. Coalowners, wanting to reap lower costs through competition among ports, supported proposals for new railway lines.

The Pontypridd, Caerphilly & Newport Railway linked the steam-coal pits of the valleys with the docks at Newport. The double-track railway was opened in July 1884 from a junction with the TVR just south of Pontypridd, crossing the Broadway and the River Taff on a viaduct. The line cut through Ynysangharad, over the Glamorganshire Canal and Pentrebach Road, and then through Glyntaff and Dynea to Caerphilly. Another section was opened in April 1886 to complete the 16 miles from Pontypridd to the Alexandra Docks at Newport. Passenger services began on 18 December 1887. The company was taken over in 1897 by the Alexandra Docks & Railway and the passenger service was run by the Great Western Railway from early in 1899. Halts were then built at Glyntaff and Dynea.

The Bute Docks Co. secured powers in 1897, after a fight with the TVR and other companies, to construct several lines in the Cardiff area and became the Cardiff Railway Co. in August 1897. Construction began of a main line from a junction with the Rhymney Railway at Heath to Pontypridd but by 1911 it had reached only as far as a junction near the Dyffryn at Rhydyfelin. The TVR pleaded in a legal battle that it would be robbed of much coal traffic by the new railway and completion of the line to Pontypridd was not approved. Rhydyfelin Halt remained the terminus, although a few trains did cross the large road and river viaduct built near the Dyffryn Arms (now the Jubilee) to steam into Pontypridd on ceremonial occasions.

Barry Railway

The Barry Railway, of great importance to Pontypridd, was born because coalowners and shippers despaired at the inability of existing railways and docks to cope with the rapidly expanding coal trade of South Wales. A bill for a Barry Docks & Railway Co. was defeated in Parliament in 1883 after strong opposition by the Bute Trustees, the TVR and others. A second battle ensued and an Act was passed on 14 August 1884. To qualify for trustee status and other benefits, the title was changed to the Barry Railway Co. by another Act of 1891.

The Act authorised an extension eastward from Cadoxton, from where the main line turned north to Pontypridd Graig (St David's) station and on to a junction with the TVR at Hafod. One branch would lead from Tonteg Junction down to the main line of the TVR at Treforest Junction to tap coal mined in the Taff and Aberdare valleys. Competition from the new railway created conflict and rivalry between the Barry and TVR that lasted for 30 years until both were amalgamated with the Great Western Railway in 1923.

Some heavy engineering work was needed to reduce gradients on the line, which also included a mile-long tunnel between Drope Junction and Wenvoe and another 1,373 yards long between Graig station and Treforest station above Llantwit Road. Navvies digging out the Treforest tunnel came across a seam of coal, and many Graig residents sorted through the thrown-out piles of debris for months to fill thousands of sacks, buckets and tin baths for their fires. The bricked-up entrance to the tunnel at the western end of the Graig station can still be seen from above the Dewi Sant Hospital in Albert Road on the Graig. A British Telecom building now stands on the site of the station.

NEWBRIDGE.

Above: Brunel's skew stone-arch bridge built in 1840 over the Rhondda at Mill Street. Later widened by building another bridge alongside. **Below:** Navvies loading boats at Foundry Bridge during an interruption to traffic following a breach in the canal.

Above: Brakes and cabs in Market Street, looking towards the Fountain area, *c.* 1904. Many of the vehicles were made in Morgan Street by the Pontypridd Coachbuilding & Wheelwright Co. The 'Silver Teapot' buildings are centre left. **Below:** Site of the Nantgarw Colliery, sunk in 1911. Now demolished, the development site is known as Brecon Gate. Nantgarw China Works in the background.

Nantgarw China Works or Pottery alongside the Glamorganshire Canal. **Above:** a wood-cut of 1868. **Below:** A late Victorian photograph.

Above: Horse and trap trotting past the Butchers Arms (Park Hotel) in Taff Street.
Below: Easter Monday Fair, April 1938, held in the Fairfield, brewer Capt. Williams's
field and now a car park, opposite the YMCA in Taff Street. Ynysangharad House
(later used as a clinic) in the park is seen in the background.

The first Barry engine worked an inspection journey from Barry to Hafod on 22 November 1888. Barry No 1 Dock opened on 29 June 1889 and the first official coal trains ran on the ceremonial opening day of 18 July. In the first full year of operations in 1890, a total of 1,753 coal-laden ships left the port. Another dock was vital and was opened in 1898.

Passenger trains started running on 16 March 1896 (Treforest from 1 April 1898) and the Barry Company secured running powers from Hafod on to Porth station to connect with the TVR trains serving the Rhondda Valleys. An extension from Barry to Barry Island opened on 3 August 1896 and thousands of trippers were attracted to the beaches and wide sand-dunes. A branch line to Barry Pier, through a 280-yard tunnel to the docks, opened in June 1899 and trippers could enjoy cruises on the pleasure steamers to Weston-super-Mare and other Bristol Channel resorts. The Barry started a passenger service from Graig station direct to Cardiff Docks (Clarence Road) on 7 June 1897 with 12 trains a day running over the GWR line between St Fagans and Cardiff by 1899. But the Barry were not competitive on this service, for they were not permitted to penetrate into the Rhondda from Graig station.

Few carriages were heated. Lighting by bottled gas was not installed until 1899 and the darkness of the two long tunnels often caused consternation among passengers. Many of the third class compartments were fitted with wooden-slatted seats which, set in the four-wheeled carriages, gave an uncomfortable ride, although more comfortable six-wheeled carriages were introduced later.

On Mabon's Day and throughout summer weekends, many mineral engines and nearly every Barry passenger coach and many belonging to other companies were pressed into service for excursions to Barry Island—except those of the TVR which had its own rival resort, and also its own large hotel, at Penarth. Both resorts were packed on every possible occasion: the Victorians of Pontypridd and the valleys liked to be beside the seaside.

Chapter 4

Hives of Industry

People bustled along the cobblestones of Market Street to the line of cabs standing in the pale gaslight. Fifteen late-nighters clambered aboard the ten-seat wagonette or brake bound for Ynysybwl. Twenty or more packed into the fourteen-seat brake for Cilfynydd and handed their fares to the boy guard perched in his iron-railed rumble seat which jutted out from the rear of the brake at the top of the steps. The driver gathered the reins of his two-horse team and urged them on. He called to the passengers (according to the *Pontypridd Observer* in October 1899): 'Get down if you see a copper!' Prosecution and conviction for overloading a brake meant at least a 5s fine and even the loss of his licence if a cabman's face became well known to the local magistrates.

The chilled and damp open-air travellers reportedly envied the comfort of a four-wheeled brougham cab coming into town, and were jealous of the passengers seen in silhouette beyond the gleaming carriage lamps of the smart hansom cab which passed them at a trot. In 1899, 57 brakes and 30 cabs operated in Pontypridd. Many of the vehicles and scores of tradesmen's carts were made in the town which, like most other towns and villages in Wales, depended greatly on its local trades, crafts and industries. Pontypridd boasted its own corn mills, saw mills, tanneries, breweries, and many hives of small industry. It was proud of its blacksmiths, farriers, wheelwrights, coopers and hosts of other craftsmen and women. It sent its heavy engineering and other manufactured goods to many parts of the world.

Coaches and Crafts

The major horse-drawn vehicle manufacturer in Pontypridd, and the largest of its kind in Wales, was the Pontypridd Coachbuilding & Wheelwright Co. based at its steam-powered carriage works in Morgan Street. Gwilym James was the manager in 1893. The secretary, William Peasley, founded the substantial Victoria Carriage Works in Ynysangharad Road. In earlier times, Morgan Street was known as Ynysgefeiliau ('field of the smithies') because of the many forges there. Except for a few houses at its northern end, the street and its small courts like Matthews Court and Cooks Place, where a nailmaker's forge once stood, have been demolished to make way for a bus station and police headquarters.

At the works teams of carriage makers and carpenters made the running gear that carried the bodywork. The wheelwright's skill turned blocks of elm into naves or hubs for the wheels, and lengths of oak into spokes. Blacksmiths forged the ironwork. From timber and steel the bodymakers constructed the brakes and cabs, two-wheeled milk floats fitted with churn racks, butchers' carts (which proved the fastest things on two wheels as they sped furiously about the town) and the four-wheeled camel-top vans used by local bakers and grocers. Some timber was grown locally but most came by rail to the goods depot in nearby Gelliwastad Road.

The coachbuilders produced mail carts, coal carts, hand carts and even wheelbarrows or 'navvy' barrows. Many tub-shaped governess carts of basketwork construction were made for families residing in the large Victorian houses dotted about the district or set in fashionable locations like Graigwen Place, Gelliwastad, Tyfica, and Merthyr Road. Two-wheeled traps and light carriages on springs, drawn by one horse, were popular private vehicles and were always on sale at Morgan Street and also on a Wednesday at the yard of the Butchers Arms where horses were also sold. Large drays were made for the local breweries. The drays, drawn by a pair of powerful Clydesdale horses in their shining harness, were a familiar sight in Victorian Pontypridd as they hauled loads of beer barrels to more than a hundred local public houses. Employees of the Pontypridd Coachbuilding Co. and their families filled a long procession of brakes, each drawn by four horses, for their annual outing all the way to Porthcawl.

The hansom cab was a two-wheeled cab for two passengers and many were made in Pontypridd. It had large wheels some 7½ft in diameter and was drawn by a single horse. The driver sat high up behind the body of the cab and the reins passed over the hooded roof with a small trapdoor through which the driver and his passengers could communicate. Entry to the leather upholstered interior was through padded knee-doors, or half-doors, at the front. Brass carriage lamps were fitted on each side of the cab. The aristocratic hansom was spruce and racy in appearance and its whirling wheels rumbled over the macadam road surfaces in Pontypridd and the district while the driver cracked his long-lashed whip in a great flourish as the horse plunged forward with its tail streaming out against the splashboard.

The Pontypridd coachbuilders employed many craftsmen such as coach trimmers for lining and upholstery, coach painters and french polishers, lampmakers and locksmiths, glaziers, embroiderers, curriers for the leather work, blind and harness makers. In August 1897 the Pontypridd Coachbuilding Co. took over the businesses of Howard Williams of Mill Street and John Doxey & Sons of nearby Rhondda Road. Some work was also passed out to the many specialist firms and individual craftsmen in Pontypridd. John Livingstone had a coach-building works in Taff Street in the 1880s and 1890s. Moses Cule was busy at his craft in Pentrebach Road from the 1850s, and George Ham was on the Graig in 1875. He was later the landlord of the Horse and Groom.

Some wheelwrights were also skilled blacksmiths, such as William Griffiths, who ran the Taff Wheel Works in Sion Street near the Old Bridge for nearly 40 years from the early 1860s and was followed by his son John. Many long-serving Pontypridd blacksmiths toiled at their forges through the Victorian years. Also important to the coachbuilding business was Thomas Reynolds, a wagon grease manufacturer at the Taff Oil Works on Tramroad.

George Hill Williams was a saddler and harness maker in Bridge Street for 40 years from 1860 and Gomer Thomas owned a similar business in Mill Street, in a workshop occupied until recently by the Swalec (formerly South Wales Electricity Board) showrooms. Gomer Thomas worked at his bench for over 30 years to cut the harness and saddles for the draft and riding horses of the town. His shop window glowed in the outside darkness of Mill Street with burnished brass and the sheen of leather in the light of oil lamps and candles.

Phillip Lougher, a tanner, currier and fellmonger, had a leather goods shop near today's Boots the Chemist for 40 years. In 1870 he opened a tannery at the Glyncoch end of Berw Road alongside the River Taff. Hides and skins supplied by local farmers and the Tramroad slaughterhouse were processed and tanned with crushed oak bark and other substances in large pits and vats. Well directed winds brought the smells from the tannery to villages close by. After being dressed, the hides and skins were turned into leather for the saddlers, upholsterers, bootmakers, glovers, bookbinders and many other craftsmen and women of Pontypridd and elsewhere. Phillip Lougher & Son carried on as leather merchants in Market Street for some decades beyond the Victorian age.

Mills

Daniel Lougher was one of several corn millers and flour merchants in the Pontypridd area. He owned the Rhondda Flour Mills—a large building erected before 1860 on a site alongside the Rhondda bridge by today's Mothercare store. Water from the river drove a wheel that worked the grinding machinery. Grain was raised to the upper floor by a hoist and released on to the rotating millstones. The flour was collected in bins and sacked and the heavy cartfuls distributed throughout the area. The mill was run by Seth Francis from about 1875. John Williams owned the Upper Mill in Millfield in the 1860s and then David Williams followed until the end of the century. The mill was situated just below Mill Street school and the mill-race extended from a weir on the Rhondda close to the Merlin Bridge to serve the mill. The mill-stream ran out under the seven-arch railway viaduct before it discharged into the river alongside the Thomas Jenkins tannery, occupied later by Humphreys Garages.

There was a water-driven corn mill by the Cross Keys public house in Nantgarw where the miller was Edward Edmunds, another at Glyncoch near Clydach Court or 'Grovers' run by Thomas Richards from about 1800, and a third near the weir in Treforest. There was another on the east bank of the ford on the Taff near the Dyffryn at Rhydyfelin from which the village takes its name ('ford of the mill'). The mill was gutted one night in a spectacular mass of flames and was not rebuilt.

Thomas Price in the 1840s and Edward Morgan in the 1860s kept the Upper Boat mill alongside the River Taff at the foot of Dynea Road. From about 1880 the miller was Enoch Griffin and the mill continued in use through the Edwardian and later years. The name Upper Boat or Baduchaf referred to one of the three boats used to ferry people across the Taff. One, known as the 'lower boat', was stationed at Taffs Well; another was at Rhydyhelyg ('Willowford'); and the 'upper boat' was moored at Bridge House near the Upper Boat Inn. At one time, passage across the river was by means only of a trapeze crossing at Maesmawr Cottages near the present-day railway halt for the Treforest Industrial Estate.

The Forest Factory at Penyrhiw on the Graig was one of three important Victorian cloth-making and fulling mills in Pontypridd. It was opened before 1850 by Samuel John Jones of Pembrokeshire. Ten men and women spun and wove woollen and flannel material and goods including blankets, quilts, shirts, shawls and dress flannels. Most operations were done by hand although some machinery was power-driven. Some finished cloth was dyed and sent together with knitted plain and fancy woollens for sale at Samuel Jones's stall in Pontypridd Market, to the Cloth Hall in Taff Street or to Cardiff for shipment to London and overseas. The factory closed in the late 1890s and the surrounding land was acquired by the Maritime Colliery Co. for tipping and the construction of washeries.

Evan James moved from Caerphilly to Pontypridd in 1844 and took over a small woollen factory in Mill Street. At this 'Ty'r Ffatri' in 1856 Evan James and James James composed the Welsh National Anthem. The spinning wheels and weaving looms were operated mainly by women and power for the factory came from a waterwheel turned by the Rhondda which runs between Mill Street and Sardis Road.

Tom Williams, a renowned tenor and the father of celebrated soprano Madame Williams-Penn, owned the Cambrian Woollen Mills in Temperance Place, situated off Taff Street by Gas Lane—an area which has now been cleared for new shopping developments. The mills were powered by a waterwheel on the Taff. David Wilson & Co. ran them for 40 years until the 1920s. After their closure, part of the premises was used by the Salvation Army as a barracks. The Ponty-pridd woollen manufacturers faced much competition from five factories producing similar goods at Caerphilly where the local fair was an important centre of the woollen trade in Glamorgan from 1850. Examples of typical Victorian cloth mills and looms can be seen today at the Museum of Welsh Life at St Fagans.

Breweries

In addition to the individual brewers and maltsters who supplied their own public houses, several large breweries in Pontypridd kept local pubs well stocked with ales, porters, stouts and beers. David Leyshon owned the Graig Brewery in Rickard Street from the 1860s, which became part of the Pontypridd United Breweries in Edwardian times. The Henry Hopkins brewery in Courthouse Street on the Graig was known as the Glen View Brewery until it became the Newbridge-Rhondda Brewery Co. in the 1890s. The typically high and narrow brewery building, last occupied by L. Slack & Son, was demolished a few years ago to make way for the new courthouse. On the Tramroad was the Station Steam Brewery of John Jabez Evans. One of the pubs he supplied was the Brynffynnon Hotel in Llanwonno and he was so charmed by its attractive location that he bought the free house in 1898 for £3,200.

The Pontypridd & Rhondda Valleys Brewery was alongside the Taff behind Boots the Chemist. Its tall chimney-stack was a central landmark for many years. It was the oldest brewery in Pontypridd and was known as the Captain's Brewery because of its ownership by Captain William Williams of Danygraig House, now the site of the YMCA. Around the brewery yard were stables for the delivery horses, store sheds for the large vats, and workshops where barrels were made by 'wet' coopers like Andrew Styles. Local 'dry' coopers made casks for goods such as Nantgarw porcelain, and 'white' coopers made wooden churns, milk-pails and washtubs.

Three local maltsters in 1850 were Lewis Davies, Amy Llewellyn and Ebenezer Williams of the Old Maltsters public house. There was a malthouse on the Graig side of Pontypridd railway station and another at Ceridwen Terrace opposite the Maltsters Arms by the Old Bridge. The smells from the malthouse wafted down Sion Street and over the open fields where Trallwn, or Trallwng, was built later. In Sion Street, the Taff Aerated Water works of Elliott & Co. made mineral waters for several decades and the John Banfield Aerated Water & Bottling Co. was busy in Ynysangharad Road and Berw Road.

Miscellany

A site on the Tramroad which was used later for the Pontypridd Public Abattoir attracted a succession of Victorian entrepreneurs. Several fires in the 1860s brought havoc to the Lewis Tar Works there, thirty years before a fire brigade was formed in Pontypridd. Tallow makers on the site included George Mellor and the Pontypridd & Rhondda Candle-works of Harry Rees. At the other end of town, James Chick was a tallow chandler and the James Richards Candleworks was situated from the 1850s to the 1880s by today's Athletic Club.

Pontypridd had two large wood distillers and manufacturers of chemicals such as acetates of lead, soda and lime, naphthas, acids, solvents, grease, pitch and charcoal. The Pontypridd Chemical Works—afterwards Alfred Chivers & Co.—was at Pontshonnorton before 1865. Supplies of wood were taken from the local hillsides and loaded on to donkeys by men and boys employed by Jotham Chivers who also founded the Cambrian Vinegar Co. in the village. The Rhondda Chemical Works alongside the road at Gyfeillon was bought in 1847 by Holloway and Smith.

Five brickworks existed between Pontypridd and Dinas by 1854. Brickworks were usually situated near a colliery. The Tymawr Brickworks of Jones Brothers in Hopkinstown made bricks for several decades with clay dug from an adjoining coal level. The Great Western Colliery Co. bought the works and constructed coolers and screens there for the Tymawr Colliery. The Victoria Brickworks, on a site which is now the playing grounds of Pontypridd Rugby Football Club in Pwllgwaun, used underclay from the No 1 Rhondda seam of coal to make large quantities of firebrick. Bricks were moulded from the clay, or pug, kneaded in a pug-mill—a large barrel fitted with knives and made to revolve by the power of a horse walking in a circular path—and then fixed either in clamps or in one of the brickworks' up-draught kilns. Coal was available from the nearby Pwllgwaun Colliery, known as Dan's Pit or Dan's muck-hole. Financial difficulties led to the Victoria works being wound up in August 1900.

Several brass and iron foundries were established before 1850 and were still in production 50 years later, including the Rhondda Foundry at Tymawr, the Coedpenmaen Foundry near the Newbridge Arms, and the Melin Corwg Foundry of Hopkin Jones near the foot of Dynea Road in Upper Boat.

There were numerous steam-powered sawmills, such as those of Thomas Evans in a yard at the bridge end of Taff Street and the Pontypridd Steam Joinery sawmills of John Henry James near the Berw railway viaduct. The largest sawmill was that of William Jones of the Rolling Mill Inn on the Graig. At timber merchant Edward Aston's Coedpenmaen Farm was one of the two boat-building docks of the village. From the early Victorian years he built canal barges, as did David Davies of Coedpenmaen, David Jones of Rhydyfelin, and Evan Davies of the Upper Boat Inn.

James Coombes was a baker and confectioner in the town for more than 40 years from 1860. His original bakery was in Mill Street near the pre-1850 bakery of Aaron Cule. Thomas James managed a steam-powered bakery in Morgan Street and the South Wales Confectionery Works produced its many delights. Thomas Mordecai and Isaac Protheroe had bakeries in Taff Street, and Hopkin Morgan ran a baker's shop there.

Hopkin Morgan was born in 1854 on the Graig where his father kept a grocery shop in the High Street. Bread was baked at the shop by his mother but eventually a bakery was built further up the hill in a building which is now a club. Hopkin Morgan later opened a large steam-powered bakery in East Street, Trallwn, and constructed a short length of canal to join the Glamorganshire Canal so that sacks of flour brought from Cardiff Docks could be delivered by barges direct to the bakery. Hopkin Morgan gave many private and public gifts. At Christmas 1897 he sent a half-ton of cake to the Cardiff Santa Claus Fund to be shared among 2,000 children in need. He became a Graig Ward councillor on the formation of the urban district council in 1895 and was chairman several times. He was also a justice of the peace.

Weekly newspapers flourished in Victorian times: in the 1870s Archibald Allan McLucas established the *Pontypridd District Herald* which was printed in St Catherine Street and Mill Street. A few years later Benjamin Davies of Mill Street brought out the *Pontypridd Chronicle* and the *Rhondda Chronicle*. These two papers later came under the proprietorship of the Glamorgan Free Press. The *Glamorgan Times* and the *South Wales Daily News* also had offices in the town. The first issue of the *Pontypridd Observer* was dated 20 March 1897 and cost a halfpenny. From offices first at 77 Taff Street, next door to the then main post office, the newspaper was edited by Percy S. Phillips until the Second World War, when D.C. Lewis and then John Lewis became the editors. The *Rhondda Leader* was born in December 1899 and the *Porth Gazette* in December 1900.

The motor car loomed on the Pontypridd horizon when in 1898 the Morris Brothers cycle business became the Cycle & Motor Car Works. In September 1899 the brothers brought a new car from London over two days of motoring. It was a phaeton-carriage type with a Crypp gear for bottom speeds so that the car could climb steep hills without the occupants having to get out and push. The first motor car in Pontypridd was owned by an Evan Thomas. In June 1898 he and the local vicar set out for a holiday at Aberystwyth and arrived in the town after a day-long 100-mile journey. The *Aberystwyth Observer* reported that the car was the first one seen there. Local people were astounded at the sight of the strange conveyance parked outside the Lion Hotel and were keen to learn how it was powered without horses. Watched by curious onlookers, the local clergy had a run around Aberystwyth in the car and 'were surprised at its speed and easy manipulation'.

Nantgarw Pottery

Fine porcelain was manufactured at Nantgarw during two periods between 1813 and 1822. A range of cheaper glazed earthenware was also produced through the Victorian years. William Weston Young chose the site and started building kilns alongside the Glamorganshire Canal which offered easy and cheap means of transport.

William Billingsley (1758–1828) arrived at Nantgarw early in 1813 from the Worcester porcelain factory. He made his home at Nantgarw House which the previous owner, farmer Edward Edmunds, had used as an inn. With a meagre capital of £250 Billingsley and his son-in-law Samuel Walker founded the Nantgarw pottery or china works. The enterprise suffered from financial instability throughout its life.

Plates were the main product at Nantgarw in the formative years but few were decorated. Dealers bought the porcelain 'in the white' and decorated it to meet the prevailing fashions. Nantgarw porcelain was known as 'artificial soft' from the nature of its paste or body which could be potted very thinly and was made to Billingsley's perfected, secret formula: a synthetic mixture of alkaline and aluminium silicates with added bone ash. Bones, burnt and mixed with clay, were ground by miller David Jones in a mill adjoining the Cross Keys public house. The waterwheel was powered by a leat running from the canal to the River Taff.

For various reasons during his Nantgarw venture, Billingsley often used the alias William Beeley. He was a celebrated painter of flowers, particularly roses, although he also painted some landscapes and shells.

At Nantgarw, Billingsley painted many dessert services, tea and coffee sets, plates, dishes and tureens; collections remain in museums throughout the world. A Worcester porcelain jug decorated with flowers and painted by him was sold by Sotheby's in June 1986 for £1,000, when it was bought by the National Museums & Galleries of Wales.

The high degree of heat necessary to produce perfect specimens made Billingsley's soft paste a difficult and sensitive body to fire. As much as 90 per cent of production, which began in November 1813, was spoiled in the firing process and taken from the biscuit kiln damaged, warped and generally unusable. Such high production losses while dependent on their small cash resources led Billingsley and Walker into financial problems. By mid-1814 they had spent their initial £250 capital and also an additional £600 advanced by Young as a partner. In September 1814, the partners petitioned for government support but were unsuccessful, despite their claim that Nantgarw porcelain was superior in quality to Dresden, French Sèvres and any British china: a claim not all collectors and connoisseurs supported, for they considered it 'lacked the soft and subtle charm of mellow warmth possessed by the older glassy porcelains'. Nantgarw, like other soft paste chinas, was a kind of glass made opaque by the addition of china clay and the perfect specimens were highly translucent with a brilliant, smooth glaze.

In October 1814 Billingsley and Walker joined Lewis Weston Dillwyn at his Swansea pottery and the Nantgarw kilns were closed down. Billingsley's formula soon proved too costly to manufacture and he concentrated on painting porcelain. Meanwhile, Young sought capital to finance the reopening of the Nantgarw works. He obtained £1,100 from unknown sources and an additional £1,000 from a number of Merthyr ironmasters. Billingsley returned to Nantgarw at Christmas 1816 and restarted production. Walker joined him in the following September. The porcelain made at Nantgarw between 1817 and 1819 was of a finer quality and design than formerly, while decoration excelled in brilliance and colour. Besides Billingsley and Walker, the best known painters engaged at Nantgarw at this time were John Latham and William Pegg who came from Derby in 1817. There were twenty other workers, ten of them children. Nantgarw china, if marked at all, bore the name 'Nantgarw' with the letters 'C.W.' added below.

Perfect specimens of Nantgarw porcelain still proved too costly to make and financial problems reappeared. The partners, and other painters, left in April 1820 to join John Rose of Coalport. Billingsley spent his remaining years there as a flower painter. Young took control and brought Thomas Pardoe (1770–1823) from Bristol where he had a china-decorating and glass-staining business. Pardoe's art embraced landscapes, fruit, birds, butterflies and other subjects. An auction of several hundred painted lots was held at Cowbridge on 9 May 1821 to raise cash to meet current expenses. The business struggled on until all remaining stocks of porcelain were sold at auction on 28 October 1822. The machinery and materials were sold to John Rose and the Nantgarw works closed down for the next ten years.

In 1833, William Henry Pardoe, the son of Thomas Pardoe, came to Nantgarw to manufacture glazed earthenware in a wide range to satisfy Victorian taste. Also in demand were clay smoking pipes and a third kiln was built for their manufacture. The pipes were made by rolling a thin body of clay for the stem which was attached to a small lump of clay for the bowl. The stem was pierced with a wire. When this roughly hand-shaped model had stiffened it was placed in a two-piece mould. The two halves were then clamped and the surplus clay squeezed out. After trimming, the pipe was taken from the mould to dry and was scraped of defects before firing. Pipes were placed in numerous racks around the kiln to become bone dry.

W.H. Pardoe made the Nantgarw works commercially successful despite long-term problems caused by shortage of labour. Children made up 70 per cent of the workforce in the 1840s. After he died in February 1867 the business was carried on by his widow and two sons under the name of Pardoe Brothers. Many clay pipes which are found today bear this name. From the end of the Victorian era the Pardoes manufactured an increasing amount of cheaper hardware as the market for earthenware declined rapidly. The demand for clay pipes was curtailed by a general increase in cigarette smoking and the popularity of French briar pipes. Production at Nantgarw finally ceased in 1921.

A great deal of Nantgarw fine porcelain was destined for display in collectors' cabinets and, for that reason, many beautiful pieces survive in perfect condition in museums and private homes. In recent years the site of the works has been excavated and conserved by the former Taff-Ely Borough Council and was was opened to the public in 1991.

Chapter 5

Heavy Industry

Besides coal mining and quarrying, heavy industry in Victorian Pontypridd was centred on four metalworking companies: the Taff Vale Ironworks, Treforest Tinplate Works, Forest Iron and Steel Works, and Brown Lenox Chainworks.

Y Gwaith Bach

The Taff Vale Ironworks, known as 'Y Gwaith Bach', was built in the late eighteenth century by either Biddulph & Co. or a Westmoreland company owned by a group of Wesleyans who erected the first chapel in Treforest. The ironworks was situated on the west bank of the Taff at Treforest and covered an area now bounded by Lawn Terrace, Windsor Road, Treforest Foundry, and the row of shops at Taff House opposite Fothergill Street. The Taff Vale Foundry of Isaac Rowlands was in the area in 1850. By 1864 the proprietors of the ironworks were Fothergill & Hankey and the manager was Charles White. Richard Fothergill was one of the principal landowners in the district. The ironworks had ten puddling furnaces and four rolling mills and several hundred men and women were employed, mainly in the production of rails for the Taff Vale and other railways.

Raw materials came from the parent Aberdare Ironworks and the Aberdare Iron Co.'s Bwllfa Colliery (Carr's) in Rhondda Fawr. Finished rails were sent by tram on a track over the company's 1851 iron bridge crossing the river to the Glamorganshire Canal which it met at a point near the old Duke of Bridgewater Arms. A footbridge crosses the river there today. Water supplies were obtained from the river and also from a small reservoir on the site of the furniture warehouse opposite Taff House. Production of iron declined after 1880 and the works closed before 1900, although a small foundry still exists on the site.

Above: View of the canal from the Common in Victorian times. St Mary's Church, Glyntaff, is on the left in the far distance. Centre is the Taff Vale Ironworks. Far right is the Forest Iron & Steel Works. **Below:** The weir and feeder channel at Treforest.

Above: Fothergill Street, Treforest, *c.* 1915. **Below:** The Newbridge Works of Brown Lenox at Ynysangharad in Victorian times, showing the two-rise staircase locks on the Glamorganshire Canal.

Above: The Round Houses, Rhydyfelin. Demolished in 1938, they stood in grounds now occupied by Pontypridd College in Dyffryn Road. **Below:** Stone Circle which once stood in the grounds of the University of Glamorgan.

Above: Furnace workers at Treforest Tinplate Works. **Below:** Forest Iron & Steel Works, Treforest, 1899. Built in 1858 by Francis Crawshay. White Tips in the background.

Tinplate Works

Victorians using the Devil's Bridge from Llantwit Road at night must have believed that the scene was painted by the Devil himself. The brilliant glare from the furnaces of the Treforest Tinplate Works below framed the angry sky and the belching black smoke on a lurid canvas of massed red and orange. The dark slopes of the Barry Mountain were brushed from a palette of sulphurous yellow and flamed with crimson, while across the flaring river the quiet hearths of Rhydyfelin and Hawthorn, with cottages like a raking of glowing cinders, flickered in shades of purple.

In 1794, Richard Crawshay, the London iron merchant who had then recently acquired Cyfarthfa Ironworks at Merthyr, bought from Christopher James of Treforest the small tin-mill situated on the west bank of the River Taff opposite the Dyffryn at Rhydyfelin. Production of tinplate continued until 1831 when William Crawshay, Richard's grandson, invested his own capital, leased additional land and erected more buildings. A recession in the industry forced a suspension of building but work resumed in 1833 and production at the modernised tinplate works began in 1835.

Management of the works was given to William Crawshay's second son Francis (1811–78), whom his father considered to be too reckless and eccentric to take charge of Cyfarthfa. The Treforest Tinplate Works failed to make a profit under Francis Crawshay's control. He was too eager to spend his time shooting at Barry Island, which he owned, and blamed the financial losses on inadequate machinery at the works. In 1842 the works consisted of some 25 furnaces, together with foundries, coke ovens and workshops. All the machinery at this time was driven by power from eight waterwheels but some steam power was used later. There are coloured drawings by T.H. Thomas of tinplate manufacture at the works in 1874 at the National Museum & Gallery of Wales in Cardiff.

The mill-race for driving the waterwheels came originally from a stream called Nant-y-Fforest, but this proved inadequate as a power source for the new machinery and so in the 1830s a weir was built across the Taff just downstream from the Castle Inn Bridge. A sluice took water to a feeder, about ten feet above the river level, which led to sluice gates at the works. Canal boats conveyed iron from the Crawshays' works at Hirwaun, in the Cynon valley, to the Machine bridge at Glyntaff where it was loaded on to trams. This tramroad followed the river just below River Street and Forest Road to the weir from where it ran alongside and above the feeder in front of Long Row, through the fields where Meadow Street was built later, and on to the tinplate works. Finished tinplate left the works on a tramroad that ran over the Julia Bridge, named after one of Francis Crawshay's daughters, and over the Cardiff Road by Janet Street to the Doctor's Canal to join the Glamorganshire Canal dock at Dynea.

To protect themselves from the searing heat, the workmen wore thick trousers, knee-length woollen stockings and leather-covered clogs. Most also wore short aprons of leather and flannel shirts with an absorbent sweatcloth round the neck. They often cooled off later with quart jugs of ale from the Dyffryn Arms across the river. Women and girls wore canvas dresses or ankle-length aprons over their woollen petticoats. They wore clogs and covered their heads with linen squares or straw bonnets. Some women spent the day separating the sharp plates; some stood with their hands immersed in baths of warm acid solution used in the pickling process; some were engaged in dipping the plates in molten tin. Women and children cleaned and polished the tinplate and did much of the heavy work of unloading and stacking the iron and coal. For twelve-hour days their weekly wage in 1842 averaged 6s 8d.

Francis Crawshay became the manager of both the tinplate works and Hirwaun Ironworks by 1855 and the sole owner of both concerns in 1856. His lack of success led to the closure of Hirwaun in 1859 and it was not until his father's death in 1867 that Francis was able to sell the tinplate works to a consortium that made the business profitable. From 1858, Francis diverted his main efforts to building an ironworks higher up the valley in the village of Treforest.

Many of the older houses in Treforest, such as Long Row and the now demolished Gwern-y-Gerwn, date from the early years of the tinplate works and their building is credited to the Crawshays. Francis is considered also to have built the Round Houses in Rhydyfelin. Their design is said to be the outcome of a wager with Francis on his ability to erect eight houses on a measured piece of land. Tradition says that the four-storey circular building with a centre courtyard about ten feet in diameter was designed with the intention of stopping housewives from seeing each other and gossiping on the doorstep instead of getting on with their daily drudgery. The names of his sons are remembered in

several terraces along Cardiff Road opposite the tinworks: Francis
Street, Tudor Street and De Barri Street. Laura Street in Treforest is
named after his wife but is nowadays more famed as one of the 'green
green grass of home' memories of international singing star Tom Jones
who once lived there.

Ironworks

In 1858, Francis Crawshay built an ironworks, originally called the
Park Works, in the grounds of Forest Isaf at Treforest, but the three
blast furnaces on what is today a football field behind Duke Street were
never put into blast during his ownership. A prominent landmark of the
village is the slag heap known as the 'White Tips'. A tramroad ran
through the tips to Kingsland Terrace and on to where New Park
Terrace is today, before sweeping round to join a tramroad running
from the southern end of the ironworks and down through Brook
Street. The tramroad branched into the grounds of Crawshay's Forest
House and also to the TVR sidings at Treforest Junction. A steam
engine on the Graig mountain near the then St Michael's Home
Orphanage above Tower Street provided power for the trams and
pumped air for the blast furnaces. Production of Bessemer steel from
molten iron began in 1873 when the ironworks and 60 acres of land
abutting the TVR lines were purchased by Sir W.T. Lewis (later Lord
Merthyr) and others who formed the Forest Iron & Steel Co. From the
1880s, steel replaced iron for railway lines made at the works.
     Supplies of coke to fire the furnaces were plentiful and came by
tramroad from Rhondda Valley collieries, including Blaenclydach
Colliery bought by the company. Water was obtained from a small
reservoir near the ironworks. The works closed in 1900 and the
furnaces and buildings were dismantled. Francis Crawshay retained
possession of Forest House and surrounding grounds and when he died
in 1878 it became the home of his son Tudor. The house became the
School of Mines in 1913. Francis placed several standing stones in the
grounds and also placed a slab bearing several Crawshay names.
Around it, Tudor erected a stone circle within a ringed grove of trees.
The stone circle was removed when the Polytechnic of Wales, now the
University of Glamorgan, was built on the site. Another ringed grove
of trees was created on the other side of the Brook Street tramroad

where Belle Vue was built.

Francis Crawshay placed other standing stones, obelisks and inscribed slabs throughout the district and in the 1840s he built a round tower, known as the Glass Tower and also as the Iron Tower, on the Graig mountain above Tower Street. It may have been used by Francis as a lodge for his local shooting expeditions. A small memorial obelisk dated 1844 and inscribed with his initials stands in a small garden in front of Castle House, once the Crawshays' offices, on the corner of Forest Road across from the police station at Castle Inn Bridge.

Chainworks

Long before Queen Victoria began her reign, Brown Lenox Chainworks were contractors to the Admiralty for chain cables and manufactured miles of wrought iron chain-links for the naval and merchant ships of many nations. The founder of the firm was Lieutenant (later Captain) Samuel Brown RN, a contemporary of Lord Nelson. After retiring from active service, Brown sought to realise his ideas for substituting chains made from iron links for the hempen ropes used for mooring vessels. Hemp ropes rotted quickly through frequent immersion in salt water and were easily cut by sharp rocks or broken in heavy seas. They took up much space on deck, needing storage in cable tiers so that they could be run out freely. For a ship-of-the-line like HMS *Victory* hempen cables could exceed 20 inches in diameter.

Brown patented a stud-link chain and in 1808 formed a partnership with his cousin, Samuel Lenox. Trading as Samuel Brown & Co. until 1823, the firm introduced chain cables to the navy in 1810. To demonstrate the superiority of wrought iron chain-cable, Brown fitted out a 400-ton ship, the *Penelope*, with her entire rigging and mooring cables made of chain and captained her on a four-month voyage to the West Indies. Chain cables were used throughout the Royal Navy by 1815. For the next century, except for a short period at the start of the Crimean War, Brown Lenox were sole contractors for chain for the navy. A new patent in 1816 covered the design of cable with improved oval-shaped links and remained virtually unchanged through the Brown Lenox history of chainmaking.

In 1812, the partners selected a site for their London works at Millwall, close to the Royal Dockyard at Deptford. When in 1818 an additional site was required, the six-acre site of Tappenden's disused nail factory alongside the canal at Ynysangharad was chosen because of its nearness to supplies of iron and coal from the valleys. Initially the 'Newbridge Chain Works', as it was known, consisted of 200 smiths' and chainmakers' fires. Eight large steam-hammers pounded away by 1900. By then, steam-driven turbines had replaced water-wheels to drive some machinery. Steam power was generally adopted at the chainworks in 1853 although in 1842 Brown Lenox became the first firm in Wales to use a Nasmyth steam-hammer. Electricity soon augmented steam power in several workshops and a foundry with electric furnaces was installed in 1922.

A small railway was laid in the works and two small tank engines were used for the movement of heavy items from shop to shop. To ease difficulties caused by congestion on the canal, a rail link was constructed in 1901 to the nearby Pontypridd, Caerphilly & Newport line to Newport Docks and a connection was also made with the TVR line to Cardiff and Penarth.

Samuel Brown patented a design in 1817 for chains that permitted the construction of larger suspension bridges. Thomas Telford later used the design for his suspension bridges at Menai and Conwy. The works produced chain for several other suspension bridges and planned and erected the celebrated chain pier at Brighton in 1823.

I.K. Brunel engaged Brown Lenox to design and manufacture the $2^7/_8$in. iron cables for the *Great Eastern* launched in 1858 specifically to lay the Atlantic cable, which she did in 1866. The great ship encountered a severe storm off Holyhead and dropped anchor. After the storm, a diver reported that the ship had been held only by the cable which was locked tightly in fissures of rock. Despite the severe strain, the chain was found to be unimpaired. Grapnels used by the telegraph cable companies for retrieving submarine cables were produced continuously at the chainworks. George James Penn was manager of the chainworks at this time and for several decades.

Although Lord Nelson's fleet consisted of so-called wooden ships, these vessels contained a large number of iron forgings. In post-Victorian years, the liner *Mauritania*'s 1,900ft-long $3^3/_4$in. cables, weighing 130 tons, were made from the scrap from some of these ships which were broken up at Penarth. The cables for the *Aquitania* in 1908 were slightly larger. Cables were supplied for several Cunard liners and for many Royal Navy warships, including the *Dreadnought*, *Nelson*, *Rodney*, *Renown* and *Hood*. Most of the German warships that surrendered at Scapa Flow in 1918 had Brown Lenox chain cables and anchors. The last major chain order was for the present-day liner *QE2*.

The mining industry had big claims on Brown Lenox and nearly every pit in South Wales was equipped at some time with bridle chains for cages, pulleys, shackles, safety hooks, tram couplings and other colliery gear. The firm was converted to a limited liability concern in 1909. In many cases, working for Brown Lenox was a revered family tradition—with the craftsmanship and skill required given by father and son for generations.

At one time, the company employed more than 500 men but fewer than 100 are employed at the chainworks today and produce crusher machinery. Much of the Ynysangharad site was cleared in early 1987 to make way for several supermarkets.

Chapter 6

Service Calls

Police

Before the passing of the County Police Act of 1839, each parish in the Pontypridd area was responsible for its own policing and the Glamorgan county magistrates appointed a resident to serve as parish constable for twelve months. He carried on with his normal occupation but had to undertake that he would discharge all the duties of a peace officer and received small fees for carrying out certain duties such as serving summonses. He did not patrol a beat but, when necessary, he led parishioners in a 'hue and cry' in the pursuit of felons. He did not wear a uniform but while on duty he carried a wooden staff as evidence of his office and authority.

The magistrates considered adopting the 1839 Act but could not agree on the formation of a police force for the whole county. Rural communities claimed that they would be unfairly burdened with rates levied to protect the growing numbers of people and properties in industrial areas like Merthyr. But the magistrates obtained approval for the appointment of a superintendent and six constables to police two divisions, one of which included the Pontypridd district. Qualifications for the appointment of a superintendent were advertised in the *Cambrian* and other Welsh newspapers in December 1839 and a Sergeant Thomas Morgan Lewis, stationed at Haverfordwest, who was a former Metropolitan Police officer and Coldstream Guardsman, was appointed and six constables were sworn in. The superintendent was paid £2 a week and the constables £1.

The constables, known as 'Peelers' in reference to Sir Robert Peel, the Home Secretary who established the Metropolitan Police, carried a wooden staff decorated with a crown at the rounded end and inscribed 'Constable' at the whorled-grip end. They wore a uniform of a black top hat, white trousers and a bright blue swallow-tailed coat buttoned to the neck and with scarlet turned-back cuffs. In place of a top hat, the flamboyant Supt Lewis chose for himself a gold-tasselled forage cap of blue with scarlet trimmings and a gold band surmounted with a gold-embroidered crown. PC Hopkin Hopkins patrolled a beat from Tongwynlais to the Moulders Arms at Upper Boat; PC John Morgan, followed in March 1841 by PC William Jenkins, patrolled from the Moulders Arms to the Duke of Bridgewater Arms on Pentrebach Road at Glyntaff; and PC Phillip Banner patrolled from the 'Old Duke' to the Travellers' Rest at Abercynon. The long and lonely beats followed generally the route of the Glamorganshire Canal and the stage coaches. The other three constables patrolled Nelson, Caerphilly and Llantrisant.

The constables faced a Pontypridd of rapid changes and increasing lawlessness. Some canal boatmen and stablemen at inns along the towpath were among those always ready to supplement meagre wages with the proceeds of robberies. Local pit-sinkers and gangs of rough hard-drinking navvies constructing the Taff Vale Railway through Pontypridd were often eager to settle their disputes by fist fights. PC Banner found his great frame and strength an advantage in his patrols round the Pontypridd railway station and the notorious pub-laced streets of Llanganna (the Graig). Major Rickards, a local magistrate, applauded the work of the constables. Other magistrates considered Supt Lewis to be a valiant officer, but the superintendent, who lived at Llantrisant, failed in his many pleas to them for a horse to help him in his supervision of a wide area. They suggested that if he lived in Pontypridd instead he would not need a horse for his kingdom.

A full county police force was formed in October 1841 and the first Chief Constable of Glamorganshire, Captain Charles Frederick Napier, was appointed. The force consisted of four superintendents, 11 sergeants and 23 constables based in four districts of Merthyr, Ogmore, Swansea and Pontypridd (Newbridge). Supt Lewis was placed in charge of the B (Pontypridd) Division. County police forces became compulsory throughout England and Wales in 1856.

The Glamorgan constables from 1841 to 1856 still wore white trousers and black top hats but the coat was now dark blue. The civilian top hat was chosen to emphasise the non-military character of the police, but the hat was strengthened to prevent its collapse under a blow. The high collar of the coat concealed a band of leather to guard against attacks with intentions of choking or garrotting. On the constable's thick silver-buckled belt hung his cutlass (when it was appropriate), a small wooden rattle to give the alarm, a lamp and handcuffs. The lamp, sold generally for oil or candle, could be shielded: it was unwise on Victorian nights to signal one's presence with a light continually showing. A policeman was issued initially with two pairs of handcuffs—one large size for men and a smaller size for women and children. A long frock coat in dark blue with a snake-buckle belt replaced the policeman's swallow-tailed coat in 1856 and the top hat was replaced in 1864 with a tall helmet, which still had a brim until 1883. The wooden rattle was replaced in 1870 by the Acme whistle: it was not possible until then to produce a whistle of distinctive tone that could be recognised as a police alarm or signal. The distinctive tone was heard repeatedly in the streets of Pontypridd.

There was no cell or lock-up in the town in 1841 and the solitary Pontypridd policeman used his house as the police station. He secured a prisoner overnight by handcuffing him to the firegrate or other ironwork in the kitchen until he appeared before the magistrate in the morning. Pontypridd was habitually crowded with thieves and vagrants. In September 1842 PC William Hume was escorting two prisoners, one a notorious Bristol thief and the other a Pontypridd prostitute, on the lonely road over Penycoedcae to Llantrisant when he was ambushed by two men who knocked him unconscious and released the two hand-cuffed prisoners into the fading light. One night in March 1843, the Pontypridd constable had to lock up 12 men in a room at the New Inn Hotel in Taff Street and sit up to guard the rowdy dozen before taking them to court in the morning. Short-term security for a prisoner awaiting the police van or a stage coach to Cardiff prison was provided by his being handcuffed to a ring used for tethering horses and found outside many Pontypridd pubs.

The constable at Nelson in 1841 also used his house in the High Street as a police station. He was fed up with guarding prisoners at night who might try to escape so he cut a hole in his kitchen wall to give access to a cell that he had built and fitted with iron rings and chains. The cell was long and low and narrow so prisoners were forced to lie prone or squat in discomfort. If an escaped prisoner was not recaptured within a month the constable in charge could be dismissed from the force. If the prisoner was recaptured the constable would be fined for serious neglect of duty.

One problem for the Glamorgan Constabulary in the 1840s was controlling the influx of unfortunate Irish families smitten by the failure of the potato crop. Hundreds of immigrants crammed on to sailing ships every week and landed secretly at lonely places on the Welsh coast. Pontypridd was inundated with stricken families, most of them making for Merthyr to seek work in the ironworks and pits. Another problem was the need for local constables to meet colleagues on neighbouring beats. The Pontypridd constable had to confer almost daily with the Nelson constable at the Travellers' Rest or at Fiddlers Elbow further on, and with the Llantrisant constable whom he met at Tir Mab Ellis which was the home of magistrate Lieut.-Col. John Hewitt on the Beddau side of Penycoedcae.

Supt Lewis left the police force in 1845 and was succeeded at Pontypridd by Thomas Mostyn. Sergeant James Thomas was the first resident of a police station completed in March 1845 in Sardis Road in Pontypridd. He was promoted to superintendent and succeeded Thomas Mostyn in January 1847, serving with distinction in Pontypridd until the 1860s. He earned commendations for his courage and leadership in the arrest of a Cardiff murderer in a Pontypridd lodging house, dealing with threatened riots at Gelligaer and a real riot in the Rhondda in 1853.

The Sardis Road police station was a single-storey building comprising three wings and three cells and was built as a lock-up for Pontypridd on a piece of land called Tir Hanna near Sardis Chapel. Dr Richard Griffiths's tramroad, which was private property, ran in front of the police station and access to the building was along a gap between the Tumble intersection and the railway station. The right-hand wing of the police station was later demolished and an upper floor added to compensate. The heavy front door of the station was lined with a thick iron sheet and secured by locks and a bar to resist forcing from outside. Every window was heavily barred, for it was not unknown for a mob to attack a police station to attempt the rescue of a prisoner.

PC William Jenkins, one of the original constables in Pontypridd, was invalided out in 1849 because of injuries received when he beat off by his sheer strength, and the flat of his cutlass, four armed men threatening to murder his chief constable at an isolated farmhouse near Velindre during the Rebecca Riots of 1843, and from further injuries he sustained in the same year when tackling rioters trying to destroy a toll-gate at Pontardulais.

Petty sessions to hear trivial cases were held by magistrates weekly on Wednesdays for many years at the New Inn Hotel assembly rooms and also at the White Hart Hotel. Magistrates attending at Pontypridd through many Victorian years included Francis Crawshay, Tudor

Crawshay and Lewis Gordon Lenox of Ynysangharad. Henry Porcher of Pontypridd succeeded John Stockwood as clerk to the magistrates in the 1890s.

In 1851, a County Court was established in Pontypridd and sat monthly at the White Hart. Judge Thomas Falconer was the first judge to be appointed locally and served for 30 years. Edward Colnett Spickett was appointed registrar in 1856 and served for more than 40 years, being followed in 1900 by J.E. Spickett. On 18 September 1863 the first sitting was held in a new County Court building (the one on the Graig, only recently vacated), built at a cost of £4,000. Judge B.T. Williams was appointed in 1882 and Judge Gwilym Williams of Miskin Manor in 1885. In 1875 Williams became the first stipendiary (paid) magistrate in Pontypridd and was followed in 1884 by John Ignatius Williams. Judge J. Bryn Roberts was appointed in 1896.

Despite the rapid growth and changing needs of Pontypridd, the police strength locally in 1852 was the same as in 1840. The town had a thousand houses and 33 beerhouses by 1852. By 1855 the population was 5,000 and following attacks on local constables an extra man came to the town in October. Five officers sent to the scene of a prize fight in that year at Llantwit Fardre between two noted pugilists were badly beaten by spectators before one of the pugilists was arrested and taken to the cells. A magistrate complained that many local vagrants committed offences such as breaking windows in the cold winter months so that they could be sentenced to prison and kept warm until the weather improved. He suggested that the offenders should have the lowest scale of prison diet: bread and water.

A new police station was built in St Catherine Street in 1868. It was commanded by Supt Jabez Matthews of Berw Road who was also the deputy chief constable of Glamorgan. In 1884 his force consisted of eight officers. The local force expanded to meet the needs and deeds of the growing population and in 1895 Supt Evan Jones had 17 officers. Supt Cole was in charge in Pontypridd in 1900 and daily drilled his officers in rifle and bayonet practice in the station yard. After more than a century of use the St Catherine Street station closed and was demolished in 1990, following the opening of a new divisional police headquarters in 1984 near the Old Bridge.

Policemen were reassuring sights to the law-abiding Victorians of Pontypridd who knew well the crimes of burglary and house-breaking. Punishment for petty offenders was usually a prescribed number of strokes of the birch rod—a bundle of about a dozen birch twigs two feet long bound together at the thick end to make a handle and left loose at the other end to form a spray. Typically, a man who stole a sovereign from a distracted Christmas shopper in Taff street in 1898 was awarded 12 strokes as, too, was a boy who stole a sovereign from his mother's purse. When she discovered the theft she promptly marched him from Coedpenmaen down to the police station while holding on tightly to his ear.

Pickpockets preyed on shoppers in the crowded Pontypridd market and bustling streets. When three women reported in 1898 that their purses had been stolen, a policeman caught two boys red-handed hiding the money in a tin in Jacob Studt the showman's field behind the Butchers Arms. One boy was punished by six strokes of the birch and the other was sent to a reformatory school for five years. A boy aged 12, one of three who held up another boy and stole his pocket-knife, suffered 12 strokes while his nine-year-old accomplices each got six strokes. A boy who stole a brass tap from the Colliers Arms in Mill Street was remanded to the Graig Workhouse as punishment. It was an unhappy start to the new year in 1900 for two boys who broke into a sweet shop and also stole china from another shop: for the first offence each boy had six strokes of the birch; for the second they were kept in prison for a week and received another six strokes on their release.

Streams of handcuffed prisoners were conveyed from Pontypridd by train or in a two-horse police van to Cardiff Gaol from where a total of 3,495 men were released in 1899. One of them was a striking miner who had served a sentence of six months hard labour for stealing a ham and ten packets of tea from Lipton's shop in Taff Street. Policemen with their lamps and lanterns patrolled the dimly lit streets and dark courts and alleys of Pontypridd where thieves and drunks and tramps often made them dangerous places to walk. Drunks arrested by the score were usually fined 10s, and a conviction for drunk and disorderly behaviour cost them £1 which was most of a week's wages. They were often sent down for between seven and 21 days in Cardiff Gaol or were sent to the workhouse. Magistrates fined a collier more than a month's wages for firing two shots from a revolver in Market Square in a drunken spree around Guy Fawkes night in 1899. During a rabies scare in Pontypridd at this time, more than a thousand summonses were served for contraventions of a muzzling of dogs order before the scare was over and the order revoked in May 1900. No case of rabies was confirmed but nearly a thousand dogs were put down in South Wales during the eight months the muzzling order was in force.

Fire

A fire brigade was formed in Pontypridd early in 1890. It operated originally from a shed in Penuel Lane near the Fountain. Its first equipment comprised one hose reel, six 50ft lengths of leather hose with brass couplings, a horse-drawn fire engine with a manually operated piston-type pump, and an escape ladder on a cart which also carried the firemen. Later, the firemen rode on a specially made horse-drawn man-cart with 'knifeboard' seating along its sides and facing outwards.

The brigade was a highly efficient unit and once attended a fire in Taff Street in under two minutes of receiving the alarm: the firemen had no time to hitch up the horses and pulled in the cart shafts themselves to reach the scene quickly. By 1894, an electrical communication from the police station sent a warning to the firemen's houses. In 1897 the brigade numbered nine strong and was commanded by Captain Arthur Owen Evans of Epworth House in Berw Road. He resigned in October 1898 and was succeeded by Captain Tom Cule. In 1898 a Sergeant Davies took charge of a hose and reel at Cilfynydd and the firemen of this detachment engaged in regular exercises by washing down the fronts of the Albion Hotel and the Cilfynydd Inn.

The Pontypridd brigade were concerned about the inadequacy and dampness of its Penuel Lane shed: by 1894 a hose and two escape ladders had become rotted and unsafe to use if fire broke out in the high buildings in the area. In 1898 the brigade were promised early possession of the old gasworks in Gas Lane for their headquarters. The firemen found the premises not only unfit but considered that time would be wasted in getting the fire engine up the hill into Taff Street. By the autumn of 1899, the alterations to make the new quarters suitable had not been made by the urban district council and all the firemen resigned at the end of October. They were not satisfied with their conditions and the lack of equipment and were angered by a councillor's allegation that they could not be considered voluntary firemen when each man received £500 a year. The correct amount was £50 which was reached after three years' service. The council accepted the resignations and invited membership of a new brigade. The strike continued until the end of January 1900 when most of the striking firemen rejoined the brigade.

In February 1900 G.V. Evans was selected as the captain of a newly organised brigade. By now their equipment included one mile of modern hose and four horse-drawn fire carts throughout the district. Hydrants in the town were few and water was often pumped from the rivers. When a fire broke out in Hopkinstown in May 1900 a fire engine was brought up to Taff Street by Captain Evans who had to wait for nearly an hour for horses. Walter Powis said his horses were ready 3½ minutes after he received instructions from the brigade. By the time things were sorted out PC Bodger said that the fire was out. But tempers still flared. The council decided to form a new brigade in August 1900 and Captain J.E. Brooks was appointed.

Steam-operated pumps later replaced the hand-operated units in Pontypridd. A young Victorian boy who was rescued from a blazing house in Market Street became a fireman himself and served under Captain Brooks: he was William Marsh of Treforest who in the early 1950s was the only surviving hand-cart fireman in Pontypridd. He remembered the Pontypridd Fire Brigade getting its first motorised fire engine in 1921 when the day of the horse-drawn fire carts had gone forever.

Ambulance

The Victorians of Pontypridd who suffered injuries, including those involved in fatal accidents, were taken by ambulance to the Graig Workhouse. One local ambulance was a single-horse 'camel top' van similar to those used by bakers. Miss Clara Thomas of Llwynmadoc (Breconshire) donated £800 to Porth Hospital so that all cases of injury in Pontypridd could be admitted there. A proposal for a Pontypridd hospital was nursed for many years but not until 1911 was the Cottage Hospital built on the Common.

Deaths occurred locally in the major epidemics of cholera in 1848, 1854, and 1866. Lime and brushes for cleansing were kept at the Pontypridd police station in Sardis Road and given out to all poor persons who asked for them. Ten of the 46 cases of cholera recorded in Pontypridd in 1866 died and there were 11 deaths from the 28 cases of diarrhoea also recorded in that year. Despite a protest by the owners of Glyncoch Mill and many inhabitants of Pontypridd in 1870, the Merthyr Local Board built a sewage treatment farm alongside the Taff just north of Cilfynydd. It caused fears of contaminated water supplies and serious outbreaks of disease. In March 1899 there were five cases of typhoid among the dwellers of 29 caravans and tents at Millfield which was also the Pontypridd 'People's Park'.

Diseases in the urban district spread because of overcrowding in school classrooms and in damp and badly ventilated houses. It took its toll because of dirty backyard lavatories, leaky cesspits and inadequate sewage disposal facilities, poor sewers and drains, and frequent pollution of the water supplies. Improperly cleansed dairies and slaughterhouses threatened dreadful consequences. Severe overcrowding in Cilfynydd houses caused several epidemics of scarlatina and diphtheria in the village. But there was no provision for the isolation of infectious diseases in the districts until April 1899 when the isolation hospital was built near Heol-y-Cawl at Tonteg.

Drinking fountains were erected in many public places in Victorian times. They were usually donated by prominent people to encourage temperance and to reduce the risks of infection from scourges such as cholera caused by drinking contaminated water. The Fountain in Taff Street was donated by Sir Alfred Thomas, the MP for East Glamorgan, in 1895. Public health was a great concern for overworked medical officers who saw the toll among both the old and the young. Of a thousand babies born in the Pontypridd district in 1899, 234 failed to survive their first year. The Vaccination Act of 1898 made it compulsory for parents to have their children vaccinated to protect against smallpox, although there were several conscientious objectors in Pontypridd who held that the vaccine would be injurious to the health of their children.

Poverty played a large and tragic part in the growth of Victorian Pontypridd. The Poor Law Amendment Act of 1834 transferred administration of the law from individual parishes to specially formed unions, each administered by an elected board of guardians who, as their first task, erected a workhouse. Outdoor relief was still given to the sick and aged poor but not to the able-bodied who would obtain relief only by entering the workhouse. Conditions within would be purposefully harsh so that the inmates would consider any kind of employment outside more desirable. Boards of guardians continued until their powers and duties were transferred to county councils in 1929–30.

Pontypridd Union was formed in January 1863 from outlying parishes in the Cardiff and Merthyr unions, including Eglwysilan, Llanfabon, Llantrisant, Llantwit Fardre, Llanwonno, and Ystradyfodwg (Rhondda). The six parishes had a population in 1861 of 30,400 which climbed to 93,500 in 1881 and reached 146,800 by 1891. A workhouse was built opposite Courthouse Street on the Graig on a site now occupied by Dewi Sant Hospital and was completed in 1865 at a cost of £9,000. The large stone structure was designed by G.E. Robinson of Cardiff to hold 320 inmates.

The first chairman of the Pontypridd Union was William Perkins and the vice-chairmen were William Pritchard and George James Penn, the manager of Brown Lenox chainworks. The workhouse master and matron until the 1890s were William and Elizabeth Johns. Edward Colnett Spickett (a solicitor and county court registrar) was clerk to the union from 1865 until his death in 1899 at his home at Bronwydd in Tyfica Road. For many years from 1880 he lived at Maesycoed House, a large residence near Maesycoed Farm, and the part of Pwllgwaun Road leading from the house down to Dan's Pit in Pwllgwaun became known as Spickett's Hill. The succeeding clerk was his deputy of many years, William Spickett. Maesycoed House was acquired in 1912 by the guardians for conversion into a children's home.

The death of an old Crimean War veteran named Jarvis in the workhouse infirmary in August 1897 and reports of other hard-working but homeless people who languished there through their last years prompted local discussion on the need, then being canvassed nationally, for a pension scheme for the aged and poor. But pensions of 5s a week for those over 70 were not introduced until 1908 when David Lloyd George was Chancellor of the Exchequer. Much was done to brighten the lives of the workhouse inmates in the late 1890s, with special dinners to celebrate the Queen's Diamond Jubilee in 1897, carols at Christmas by the local male voice choirs, and regular concerts which included artistes such as soprano Madame Williams-Penn, who was one of the soloists at the National Eisteddfod held in Pontypridd in 1893.

Pontypridd Union also had its cottage homes for children at Church Village in the late Victorian years. The large buildings (some recently demolished) are now known as Garth Olwg. During the Second World War a Royal Air Force hospital was built on an adjoining site and it was later greatly extended to become the present East Glamorgan Hospital. In 1898 there were 90 boys and girls at St Michael's Catholic Homes above Tower Street in Treforest, an orphanage and certified poor law school, originally for girls only, where Sister Illtyd Morgan was the superintendent entrusted with care of the children.

Postmarks

It was penny black and twopenny blue when the Post Office came to Pontypridd in 1840. The office was kept by a grocer named Thomas or Morris on Pentrebach Road, Treforest, and all letters were delivered and collected from there. Before the Taff Vale Railway arrived mail for the town came by riders on horseback and to the Duke of Bridgewater Arms by coach until it stopped running between Merthyr and Cardiff in 1843. A heavy parcel could be sent by coach from Pontypridd to Cardiff for 1s, while a passenger paid 2s. Mail for the Rhondda was at first collected by a famous local character known as 'Shon Waun Adda' who carried the letters in a donkey cart. Later, letters were dispatched by coal trams on the Treforest to Dinas tramroad. In 1858 the post-master introduced horse-riders to carry the mail to the valley.

Charles Bassett was appointed postmaster at Pontypridd in 1843. He started business a few years earlier as a chemist and bookseller in Taff Street in premises occupied later by Boots the Chemist. He later became manager of the Provincial Banking Corporation and gave evidence in 1844 to the Royal Commission investigating the causes of the Rebecca Riots, an attack on the excessive number of toll-gates on the roads of South Wales. One local toll-gate was cut down and farmers from Eglwysilan protested that they had to pay tolls twice before entering Pontypridd, once at a gate near the Llanover Arms and again at the Crossbrook gate in Taff Street. Charles Bassett and others founded the first permanent Wesleyan place of worship in Pontypridd at Chapel Street, though use was made earlier of an old warehouse behind today's Barclays Bank in Taff Street. He died in 1887 at his home at 'Brynffynnon', Merthyr Road.

The town's postmaster in 1875 was George Hughes and he was followed before 1880 by Alfred James MacMurray. The post office was situated in Market Street until it moved to a new main office at 76 Taff Street. From its offices next door the *Pontypridd Observer* often scolded the men who used to sit and smoke and loll about for hours on the wide steps opposite, spitting tobacco juice which stained the long dresses of the ladies who swept by.

William Key acted as sub-postmaster at his chemist shop at 90 Taff Street in 1894. At this time, David Jones was the sub-postmaster at Cilfynydd which the Post Office originally wanted to call Albion Town until the villagers organised a petition to reject the proposal. John Robotham kept the Treforest post office for more than 40 years from mid-Victorian times.

Some 25 postmen were employed in Pontypridd by 1898, ten of whom lived in Treforest. George Bartlett, who had then retired after serving as a postman for 37 years, remembered the days when two men could deliver all the local letters. In 1900, the Pontypridd Post Office Choir was well known in the area. There were three deliveries of letters daily and one on a Sunday. Callers could collect their letters at the post office at any time during its working day from 7 a.m. to 9 p.m. A new, extra mail service to the Rhondda in 1899 gave a 9 a.m. dispatch of letters which meant that someone in Pontypridd who received a letter from the Rhondda in the early morning delivery could have a reply delivered to the sender the same morning.

A local postman earned 18s a week in 1897. Because of his cheerfulness and friendliness, the postman earned a special respect throughout the community. His famous postman's knock, a rat-tat on the door knocker, announced his arrival. If he had a registered letter or a package to deliver he gave a double rat-tat as a signal for someone to come to the door. Parcels were delivered in a horse-drawn van protected inside by a wire mesh frame. Telegraph boys in neat uniforms and pillbox hats either sprinted on foot or sped on bicycles to deliver their news and also gave a double rat-tat on the door before racing back to the post office for the next message. There were few telephones in Pontypridd in 1897 but telegraph poles soon spread along the local roadsides. Thousands of telegrams were handled each year and behind the post office counter was a pneumatic tube for sending the telegrams upstairs to the forwarding rooms.

Gaslight

The streets of Pontypridd were lit for decades by gas-burner lamps which flamed and flared with a poor yellow light. But after the urban district council had experimented in February 1898 and found that two of the new incandescent 'mantle' lamps lit the council chamber more brightly than the 13 gas-burners previously used, they decided to fix single incandescents in all lamps on main roads and residential streets and double incandescents at road crossings and other places of danger.

Lighting gradually improved from 1899 but there were few gas lamps on the main roads to the outlying villages. The roads were eerie places after dusk or when only an occasional glimmer of cart lamps loomed out of the mist or fog and a vague shape with its jingle of harness and rumble of wheels broke the scary stillness and silence. There were no lights on the lonely stretch of road from Hawthorn to Upper Boat even in 1898 owing to the lack of money to lay gas pipes. Brilliant white acetylene gas lighting was pioneered locally in 1898 by Parsons' bakery in Coedpenmaen.

Gaslight was as big a topic for discussion in Victorian Pontypridd as the weather. Generally, lamps were lit at dusk, put out around midnight and lit again before dawn. But not always: some lamps were left on all night; some in the town were put out in the early hours when protection, residents in Gelliwastad protested, was particularly needed against thieves and burglars; some were not lit early enough in the morning when colliers were going to work, and anger erupted when a cart showing no lights ran into a group of men going to the Albion Colliery; and some, especially in Trallwn, never seemed to be lit at all.

Lamplighters were urged to report a defective lamp so that the local caretaker could get a ladder to rectify the fault. Caretakers complained that lamplighters could have fetched a ladder themselves if they cared enough. Residents of Berw Road used to complain that lamps on The Parade across the river were always lit before theirs. Lamplighters retorted that they could not light all lamps at once and pointed out that they worked seven days a week but were only paid a maximum of 23s for a six-day week. The TVR stationmaster at Pontypridd complained about the quality of lighting at the station which was to blame for several injuries to passengers, and oil lanterns often had to be brought so that platform brawls could be seen more clearly!

The Pontypridd Gas Light & Coke Co. was incorporated by Act of Parliament in 1850 and the local works built in Gas Lane off Taff Street. Pontypridd had gaslight for the first time on 22 January 1851 when newspapers reported that it shone on streets of 'mud, mud, and still more mud'. The first manager of the gasworks was Henry Biggs Lawrence who served for 25 years. The undertaking was taken over by the local board in 1893 and a large new works was built shortly afterwards at Glyntaff where it remains. Little cooking was done by gas and there were only 105 gas stoves in the district in 1895: the coal-fire heated ovens still reigned supreme in both terraced homes and grander houses.

The Pontypridd Electric Lighting Co. proposed in August 1899 to light the town with electricity and placed three demonstration lamps near the New Inn Hotel. Councillors were not impressed and initially blocked the scheme. In September 1900, however, they decided to obtain powers from the Board of Trade to supply electricity for public and private purposes throughout the district, although gaslight remained for decades in many streets and homes.

Pontypridd was governed from 1874 to 1895 by a local board of 12 members from offices at 56 Taff Street. Its chairman in 1884 was the Revd David Watkin Williams JP of 'Fairfield' in Hawthorn. The first members were Francis Crawshay, Aaron Cule, Moses Cule, David Davies, Jabez Evans, William Griffiths, Henry Hopkins, David Leyshon, David Morgan, Lewis Wayne Morgan and George James Penn. The clerk was Lieut.-Col. Henry Llewellyn Grover of Clydach Court near Glyncoch. He joined the Rifle Volunteers (19th Glamorgan) at Pontypridd in 1868 and when he died in 1898 his body was conveyed to Glyntaff Cemetery on a gun carriage drawn by four black, plumed horses and attended by officers and men of the 3rd Battalion of the Welsh Regiment, of which he had been in command at the Trallwn headquarters.

Pontypridd Urban District Council was formed in 1895 under the Local Government Act of 1894 when parts of six local parishes were united to form a civil parish and urban district. The adjoining Ystrady-fodwg UDC became the Rhondda UDC in July 1897. Pontypridd UDC took over the local board offices and the district was divided into six wards, each of which elected three councillors who met fortnightly. The first members of the urban district council in 1895 were James Roberts (chairman); David Richard Evans, William Seaton and William Williams (Town Ward); Hugh Bramwell, Patrick Gowan and Horatio Maynard Rowland (Rhondda Ward); David Leyshon, Hopkin Morgan and James Edward Spickett (Graig Ward); Fred Edwards, Thomas Taylor and Watkin Williams (Trallwn Ward); William Gronow,

William Lewis and Thomas Williams (Cilfynydd Ward); and Richard Thomas Richards, James Roberts, and Theophilus Richard Hamlen-Williams (Treforest Ward). The clerk was Henry Llewellyn Grover, Church Street. James Roberts continued as chairman until 1897–8 and was succeeded over the next four years by Patrick Gowan, Richard Richards, Hugh Bramwell and Hopkin Morgan.

The population of Pontypridd in 1847 was estimated at 2,000. In 1891 the population of the urban district was 20,000 and the estimated population of the whole civil parish of 8,000 acres was 30,000. It grew steadily: in October 1898 the total was 37,000 and in 1899 reached 38,000. There were then 6,000 houses in the area at an average weekly rental of 5s. By January 1901, when the population of Glamorgan stood at 880,000, that of Pontypridd was 42,000. Cilfynydd had a population of 4,500 and a total of 6,500 people lived on the Graig, one of Pontypridd's oldest villages. It was formerly known as Llanganna after an old lady who owned much property there. She was called 'Catws Llanganna', from Llangan near Cowbridge.

For parliamentary representation from 1885 to 1918, Pontypridd was included in the East Glamorgan division, for which Sir Alfred Thomas (elevated to the peerage in 1912 as Lord Pontypridd) was MP from 1885 to 1910 and A. Clement Edwards from 1910 to 1918. After a reorganisation in 1918 the Pontypridd, Llantrisant and Cowbridge districts were formed into a new division and Lieutenant Tom Arthur Lewis was elected as the constituency's first Member of Parliament. The present MP for Pontypridd is Dr Kim Howells who succeeded the late Brynmor John. Two other local men are also currently at Westminster: Lord Merlyn-Rees of Cilfynydd (previously Merlyn Rees MP, a former Northern Ireland Secretary and Home Secretary) and Lord Prys-Davies, a Pontypridd solicitor.

On the Ponty Buses

The Pontypridd & Rhondda Valley Tramway Co. Ltd was incorporated in 1885 to operate a horse-drawn tramcar service between Pontypridd and Porth. The company met financial difficulties after building the three miles of tramlines and passing loops and by late in 1887 only one tramcar had been purchased. Terms were agreed under which Solomon Andrews & Sons, who ran a horse-bus and tramcar service in Cardiff, would operate the tramway from a depot opposite Edmund Street in Porth to the Pontypridd terminus at the original Welsh Harp Hotel near Mill Street school.

The service was due to start in November 1887 but tramcars with wheels of the correct gauge could not be found and the opening was delayed until 26 March 1888 when five tramcars ran throughout the day. By January 1889, six tramcars and 21 horses were working on the route, each tram averaging five return trips every day. Two horses pulled the tram which was an open-topped double-decker with open, iron staircases at front and rear. The top deck had 'knifeboard' seating on which passengers sat back to back and looked out over the sides. They faced a wretched journey in lashing rain, and umbrellas blew inside out in the gusts of wind that often carried a sprinkling of coal dust to leave black rivulets down noses and cheeks.

Revenue from fares did not provide a worthwhile income for the under-capitalised tramway company, which went into liquidation and was bought in August 1891 for £2,000 by the South Wales Property, Machinery & Carriage Co. Ltd, a new company formed by Solomon Andrews. This concern operated the tramway profitably for several years but it was not considered a thriving business. One reason was that the permanent way or road bed for the trams was in a poor condition. The macadamised road surface had worn down to as low as three inches below the rails in places and many people and carts using the road were involved in accidents. Danger also lurked in other places where unskilled paving had left the road surface an inch above the rails. Surveyors' reports to the Board of Trade in October 1891 resulted in an order being issued for pitching or paving between the rails and for 18 inches on either side at an estimated cost of £6,000.

The tramway was sold in September 1898 to the British Electric Tramway Co. Ltd for £12,000. The sale included eight trams, 40 horses and freehold premises at Porth. Over the next few years there was great local opposition to the proposed electrification of the tramway and many petitions asserted that it would be impossible or dangerous to run electric trams along the streets. The horse-trams continued running until April 1902 when the service was withdrawn. The TVR put on 35 new coaches to cope with the increased number of railway passengers. In July 1902, 36 of the tramway horses were slaughtered at Llwyncelyn, Porth. A few horses confirmed by vets as suffering from glanders were sold for two sovereigns each while BET got market value for the rest.

Above: Electric tramcar in Edwardian Pontypridd. The errand boy stands by Danygraig House, later the site of the YMCA, in Taff Street. The horse and cart are by the Tredegar Arms; just beyond is Crosswell's Wine Shop built on the site of an old toll-house. **Below:** Electric tramcar near the Fountain. The photograph, of *c.* 1905, was taken from the steps of Penuel Chapel.

Police Superintendent Evan Jones in 1891.

Drinking fountain in Penuel Square, Taff Street.

Above: The Cottage Hospital on the Common, 1991. There was no hospital in Victorian Pontypridd. Miss Clara Thomas donated £800 to Porth Hospital so that all cases of injury in Pontypridd could be admitted there and not to the Graig Workhouse. The Cottage opened in 1911. **Below:** Wesleyan Church, now the Municipal Hall.

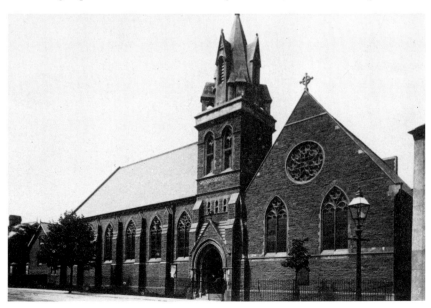

Above: Gelliwastad Road, *c.* 1899. **Below:** Horse-drawn tramcar on the Pontypridd to Porth service.

Above: Pontypridd Fire Brigade, formed in 1890. **Below:** Cardiff Road, Rhydyfelin, looking northwards in 1910.

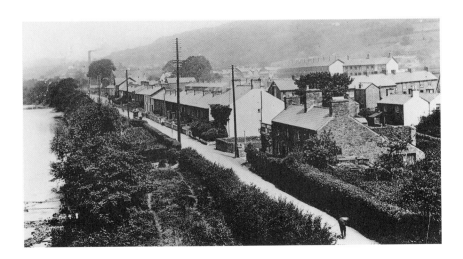

Above: Welsh Harp, old and new, Mill Street, *c.* 1904. **Below:** Berw Road, showing Tabernacle Chapel and long-demolished houses, *c.* 1899.

Above: Rhondda Bridge, High Street, showing the Temple of Fashion and progress of the Fire Brigade, *c.* 1900. **Below:** Gas works and cemetery at Glyntaff, *c.* 1899.

The Local History Collection at Pontypridd Library retains one of the 14in. by 9in. enamel plates which lists hansom cab fares operating in Pontypridd during the late Victorian and early Edwardian years:

The Urban District Council of Pontypridd

FARES FOR HANSOM CABS

(Approved by the Council on the 22nd October 1901)

FARES FOR DISTANCE

From	To	Fare
Centre of Town	Clydach Court	2.0.
Barry Railway Station	Berw Bridge	1.0.
Taff Vale Rly Station	Lock Terrace, Merthyr Road	1.0.
"	Bonvilston Hotel, Coedpenmaen	1.0.
"	Commercial Hotel, Cilfynydd	2.0.
"	Trehafod Hotel, Trehafod	2.0.
"	Holly Bush, Hopkinstown	1.0.
"	Farmers Arms, Hafod	1.6.
"	Brynhyfryd, Graigwen	1.0.
"	Graigwen Farm	2.0.
"	Glyntaff	1.6.
"	Farmers Arms, Pentrebach	1.0.
"	Barry Station, Treforest	1.6.
"	TVR Treforest (Wood Road route)	1.0.
"	Penycoedcae	2.6.
"	Graig Hotel, Graig	1.0.
"	Centre of Upper Boat village (Methodist Chapel)	2.6.
"	Dyffryn Arms, Rhydyfelin	2.0.

FARES FOR TIME

Up to 10 o'clock p.m.	First Hour	2.0.
	Second Hour	
	Every Subsequent Hour	1.6.

Licensed drivers are requested to remain out to convey passengers to and from the 8 p.m. trains.

(By Order) C. Sydney Watson
Clerk to the Council

   Long before the horse-trams, a two-horse omnibus service ran daily between Cymmer and Pontypridd. The buses met all trains arriving at the Pontypridd TVR passenger station from 1860, several years before passenger trains started running from Pontypridd to the Rhondda. In later years, wagonette brakes left every 15 minutes from Pontypridd to Cilfynydd and Ynysybwl. In 1899 there were 57 brakes and 30 hansom cabs and brougham carriages serving Pontypridd. A proposal by the Swansea Motor Omnibus Co. in June 1899 to run a Daimler motor car service between Pontypridd and Cilfynydd was rejected and horse-drawn brakes continued on the route until March 1905 when electric trams started running between Cilfynydd and Treforest, and between Pontypridd and Trehafod, and the age of the horse-brakes gradually came to an end.

   Although electric trams started running in Pontypridd in the first years of the Edwardian age, their introduction played an important part in the life of the Victorians. They were accustomed to horse-drawn transport and the electric tram had a great affect on their lives and on those of the future generation in Pontypridd. The UDC wanted and fought for a publicly owned electric tram service and Acts of Parliament of 1901 and 1902 authorised construction of the tramway. The Board of Trade examined the estimated costs of £60,000 to introduce the service and another £50,000 for a generating station to power the service and the new street lights. They believed that a private company could better serve the community and cut the huge costs. After a public inquiry in 1903, the council secured the rights to run the service and a generating station was built next to the gasworks in Treforest.

   A tram route was planned to run the 3½ miles from Treforest and through Pontypridd to Cilfynydd to be followed immediately afterwards by an extension for the 1½ miles between Pontypridd and Trehafod, terminating at the Trehafod Hotel. The firm of Blackwell, under manager Robert Grigg, started laying the tramlines in September 1903. The Treforest–Cilfynydd tramlines ran from the former council depot at Glyntaff, down past the Llanbradach Arms to Castle Inn Bridge, over the Taff, and up Forest Road. Double tracks (like those in Taff Street) or single tracks with loop-line passing points ran down Fothergill Street and along the Broadway to the Tumble, or Station Square, in Pontypridd. The trams continued down the High Street past the old and squat Clarence Hotel and the Royal Clarence Theatre, through the bustling narrowness of Taff Street and over the Victoria Bridge, up the Corn

Stores Hill to Coedpenmaen and along Coedpenmaen Road to 'The Swamp' to Pontshonnorton, to Quarry Siding and the terminus opposite the Albion Colliery in Cilfynydd. A single track loop-line was laid through Market Street in Pontypridd.

The tramway gauge was 3ft 6in. and the tramcars 6ft 3in. wide. Most of the route was lit by electricity, with 40 arc lamps set in bell-like covers fixed to the top of the tramway poles. Trams were allowed to travel at 8 mph through the town and 12 mph elsewhere on the route. A single-decker could carry 30 passengers and a double-decker 60. The double-deckers had wide, open platforms at front and rear and staircases to an open, top deck (later covered in) with forward-facing seating surrounded by guard rails fitted with wire mesh. There was a 7½-minute service through the town and a 15-minute service to Treforest and Cilfynydd. Fares were initially 1d from the TVR station to the Old Bridge and 2d to Cilfynydd.

The new tramway services encouraged more people to come into the town and market. J.E. Teasdel, the tramways manager, reported that on the first day of operation the trams carried 9,000 passengers and during the first week took more than 44,000 pennies (£183) in fares. Takings dropped after the initial novelty of travelling by tram wore off but weekly takings often reached 40,000 pennies for many years. Horse-brake services were soon badly affected by a drop in passenger numbers and many cabbies became drivers or conductors on the new trams. Horse and cart drivers in the town apparently got used to the presence of the trams quite early and horses of local traders were shifted so often when trams came along that they soon learned to do so without being told. A cross-over line in Taff Street enabled the trams 'to dodge the grocers' carts and cars admirably'. There was a new vogue for children—seeing how far they could go hanging on to a tram before being spotted and threatened by a policeman or being cursed at and thrown off by the conductor.

The Treforest–Cilfynydd trams ran for 25 years and were replaced on 18 September 1930 by trolleybuses. Tramlines were torn up and virtually removed from the whole district by the end of 1933. The operation of tram services from Pontypridd to Trehafod had always been difficult because of frequent road subsidence and flooding on the route beyond Hopkinstown. Petrol-driven buses took over on this route. The tramcars were dismantled and their wooden seats sold at 1s 3d each for use in gardens. Trolleybuses served Pontypridd for many years but in 1956 the UDC decided that the provision of new street lights and the attendant road works at Cilfynydd would mean costly alterations to the overhead electricity supply system. The trolleybus service therefore came to a sudden stop on Thursday 31 January 1957. There was a great sense of loss in the town when the last Pontypridd trolleybus, like the electric tram, returned to the depot and passed into history with the horse-drawn brakes.

Chapter 7

Face of Coal

Sixty-three miners died when fire and smoke swept through the Hetty Pit of the Great Western Colliery at Gyfeillon, near Hopkinstown, on Tuesday, 11 April 1893. There was no explosion and nearly all the victims suffocated in the smoke. Sparks were always thrown off by the strain on a wooden brake that checked the journeys or lines of coal trams going to the pit bottom down a steep gradient known as the east side hard-heading of the Hetty. The engine house overhead was draped with a brattice cloth to keep out draughts. Sparks ignited the cloth. There was no emergency supply of water nearby that day and the fire took hold and quickly spread for nearly a mile along a level called Bogey Dip and then on to the Top Parting.

Arthur Williams, a collier's boy, and his brother Tom of Queen Street, Treforest, were waiting at the end of the level for a haulier to bring some trams. Phillip Jones and a fireman came up the coal face from the next stall and said they could smell burning. Shouts from miners lower down warned that smoke was billowing along the level. The men, joined by Jack Cummings of the Graig, Charles Barber of Pentrebach Road, and Bill Atkins, a Salvation Army bandsman of Queen Street, tried escaping through the return workings of the Tymawr Pit and the Four-Foot landing. When the rescue cage came close to the men, they had to shout instructions to the hitcher at the Tymawr Bottom some 80 yards lower down. The men escaped, except for Phillip Jones who suffocated in the thick smoke on the landing along with Charles Cavell and some other men who had crawled there. One man tried to escape by leaping from the landing on to the cage but he missed and plunged to the bottom of the shaft.

The colliery was well ventilated and many miners in front of the smoke managed to escape. They reached the surface to find the colliery yard packed with hundreds of anxious relatives who peered at them searchingly in the hope of recognition. The onlookers were given more hope when after four hours a group of 62 men and boys were brought up after being trapped at the coal face. They had stumbled through the smoke to safety after protecting themselves by soaking their scarves in a pit-horse trough of water and covering their mouths and noses. The manager William James and other officials and rescuers went down the pit to help in clearing the falls that had followed the fire. The bodies of the dead miners were brought up throughout the week.

Winning the Coal

A level was opened at Gyfeillon in 1790 by Dr Richard Griffiths, the man who constructed the tramroad from there to Treforest, built the Machine Bridge and cut the 'Doctor's Canal' from Treforest to Dynea. Yorkshireman John Calvert sank the first shaft at Gyfeillon in 1848 and struck the famous No 3 Rhondda Seam which was the nearest to the surface in the valley. To celebrate the opening of the pit, he gave his workmen and their families a feast at which an ox was roasted. A print depicting the festivities and captioned 'Celebrating the winning of the coal' was featured in the *Illustrated London News* of 23 August 1851. Shortly after the opening of the pit, a battery of coke ovens was set up at a cost of £17,000 and the Tymawr Colliery was sunk.

Large quantities of coke were sent to Bristol under a contract with the Great Western Railway. John Calvert faced a large bank overdraft by 1854 and was forced into an agreement by which the GWR worked the colliery for a three-month trial period. The colliery was sold to the GWR in 1864 for £31,000 and became the Great Western Colliery. Following the resale of the colliery to John Calvert in 1874, the pit was sunk down to the steam-coal seam in 1875. Hugh Bramwell was the agent there in the 1890s.

Earlier, in 1844, John Calvert had sunk the small Newbridge Colliery high up in the Gelliwion valley above the Graig. He found good quality coal at a depth of 54 yards and installed a beam engine for winding, for which Brown Lenox made a new cylinder in 1861. The engine worked until 1918 when it was presented to the School of Mines at Treforest (now the University of Glamorgan). The nearby Penyrhiw pit was part of the Newbridge-Gelliwion Colliery Co. As a young man, Calvert had a contract for constructing part of the Taff Vale Railway and in 1841 took over and completed the branch from Pontypridd to Llancaiach. He was a generous man but reckless in his spending: at one time he lived at York House, a fine local residence, but died in comparative poverty in a Llantwit Fardre cottage in 1890.

The first pit in the Gelliwion valley was sunk in 1841 by John Edmunds of Groeswen and was later worked by Thomas Fowler & Brothers. It subsequently became the Maritime Colliery, situated in front of Woodland Terrace in Maesycoed. The upcast shaft in 1900 still had a wooden head-frame sited between two engine-houses, one of which contained the winding-engine. Steam was generated in boilers outside the second house containing an engine that operated a Waddle ventilation fan: a large open-running centrifugal fan of narrow width which drew exhausted air from the mine. A young girl playing nearby in October 1897 was caught up in the spindle of the fan and killed. Part of the coal output of the Maritime Colliery, like that of the Penyrhiw Colliery, was brought down to Pontypridd on a tramroad to a small siding at the north end of Pontypridd TVR station and 'tumbled' from a primitive chute into railway wagons, and also into trams which proceeded from the Tumble area down the Tramroad to Treforest

The Maritime shaft was sunk a short distance from Maesycoed Farm and John Edmunds found good house-coal within 50 yards of the surface. The centuries-old farmhouse squatted solidly at the end of a narrow lane that bridged the Gelliwion stream in pasture land cut from thickly wooded hillsides. Nephews of Dr Richard Griffiths owned the upper part of the Gelliwion valley and Colonel Vaughan Lee of Pwllgwaun the lower part near the farm. The *London Star* of 26 January 1804 advertised the sale of valuable timber for ships of the Royal Navy and included one lot of 422 large oak trees growing in the Maesycoed and Pwllgwaun areas.

One massive oak dominated the road from Samuel Jones's Forest woollen factory to Maesycoed Farm. The tree cast its shadow on the playing fields of the Maritime Rugby Football Club, considered to be one of the best teams in Wales in the 1880s. The club amalgamated with Pontypridd RFC in 1892. Maesycoed Farm became a highly desirable building site at the turn of the century and Rosser Street was named after a builder who discovered that the big tump from which spectators watched the Maritime RFC matches consisted of sand and sea shells, a useful building material. The first houses in Mound Road and Woodland Terrace were completed about 1908.

The entire output of the Maritime Colliery for the seven years from 1875 was sold under contract to the GWR who subsequently acquired the colliery and worked it for ten years. Following several explosions in Welsh collieries, the GWR sold the Maritime which, after further changes in ownership, was taken over in 1893 by the Great Western Colliery Co. Early this century the company employed more than 3,500 men in its six pits, all within a mile radius: the Maritime, Penyrhiw and Tymawr, and at Gyfeillon the Hetty and the Great Western Nos 2 and 3. In 1909 upcast and downcast shafts were sunk in a steam-coal area previously undeveloped about a mile from Llantwit Fardre near Cwm Farm. The Cwm Colliery was to employ 2,000 miners in two pits named Mildred and Margaret and would increase the output of coal from the local Great Western collieries to two million tons a year.

Thomas Powell was one of the principal landowners in the Pontypridd area. Although his more important ventures were at Gelligaer and in the Cynon valley, which led to the formation of the Powell Duffryn Co., he won coal from several pits and levels in the Llantwit Fardre district. He built Ida House, now demolished, and the Ida and Llantwit collieries became the responsibility of his son and namesake. Many trial shafts were sunk in the area, like those at Dyffryn Dowlais and Dyffryn Llantwit. The Taff Llantwit Colliery down the road from the Cross Inn public house was connected by tramroad to the Llantrisant branch of the TVR near the Church Village railway station. Most had closed by the end of the nineteenth century.

The opening of many mines in South Wales from 1840 created a need for labour which was not available in sufficient numbers locally. Farm workers who earned 8s a week left Somerset, the Forest of Dean, Carmarthenshire and elsewhere to earn from 16s to 18s a week in the pits. The harshness of the early Victorian years found women and girls employed down the pits for a mere 3s a week until the Coal Mines Act of 1842 brought new regulations and better conditions. Coalowners had employed boys as young as seven years of age as door-boys underground at a wage of 6d a day plus a small allowance for candles. If the boys wanted more candles they had to pay for them.

Daniel Thomas sunk the Pwllgwaun Colliery in 1872. It was known as Dan's Pit until its closure by the National Coal Board in 1948. It stood in a small field off Pwllgwaun Road leading from the Merlin Bridge and adjoined the present-day playing fields of Pontypridd RFC. In his youth, Daniel Thomas was a renowned lightweight boxing champion but he became fervently religious and burnt the belts he had earned for his victories in the ring. He helped many small local chapels with generous cash donations. He had an interest in Mynachdy Colliery at Ynysybwl. He retired in 1898 and passed the ownership of Pwllgwaun Colliery to his son-in-law William Henry Mogford of Mogford & Phillips who worked a coal level nearby.

A major pit, the Lady Windsor, was sunk at Ynysybwl in 1885 and the hillsides of Pontypridd were dotted with levels, small collieries, trial shafts and air shafts. On the Graig, John Edmunds worked the Forest Fach level from 1838 and the small Victoria Colliery was sunk above Maesycoed Farm. Lan Colliery was situated across the River Rhondda opposite Henry Street infants school. At Pwllgwaun, Seaton's Level cut into the Lan hillside and 30 men worked it for more than 20 years. Clay from the workings was used by a small brickworks on a site occupied in more recent years by a glass factory.

Several levels were opened at Penygraigwen near the engine house that served the tramway from Tymawr Colliery; there were others along from Maesyderi and more around the Lan Wood quarry from where a long tramway ran down through the woodlands and past Lan Wood or Coed-y-Lan schools. The Darenddu Colliery, near a small quarry and above Darran Park by Coed Craig-yr-Hesg, opened in 1842. High above Glyntaff coal was extracted from a level below Bryn Tail farm. The Dynea Colliery Co., managed in 1895 by Daniel Thomas, had two levels above Masefield Way in Rhydyfelin. A third entered the mountain alongside the Nant Caecorrwg stream by the old Pant Drain farmhouse nestling in its hawthorn hollow below Eglwysilan Church. Dynea No 4 was lower down the hillside near Dan-yr-Allt. Another disused level is high on the hillside below Cwrt-y-Celyn farm. John Brockett Grover's Maesmawr Colliery at Upper Boat was linked to the Glamorganshire Canal by a half-mile tramroad.

Morgan Thomas worked coal in the eighteenth century at Graig-yr-Allt Colliery beyond Nantgarw. It was owned in Victorian times by Thomas Booker & Co. They also owned the Melingriffith Tinplate Works and the Pentyrch Ironworks which was owned in the 1830s by Richard Blakemore. About 1800, one of the upper seams of coal under the Garth mountain near Pentyrch caught fire and burned for years. Apparently, if one poked a stick into the ground then flames and smoke would rise from the hole. Folklore has it that a hunter stalking the area sank up to his armpits in the soft ground and was badly burned before he was pulled clear.

At the northern outcrop, William Williams opened the Bodwenarth Colliery at Pontshonnorton in the 1870s. At Cilfynydd, several trial shafts were sunk in Cilfynydd Farm fields behind the present-day

Wood Street. Cilfynydd Red Ash Colliery was situated above Bryn Road and there was also a small brickworks near Pleasant View, later renamed Jonathans Terrace. David Griffiths was manager of Wern Ganol Colliery at Llanfabon in 1880, in a district in which there are references to coalmining as early as the 1280s.

Rhondda Bound

Walter Coffin was the principal Rhondda coal proprietor in the early Victorian years and before. The son of a prosperous Bridgend tanner, he bought a farm in Dinas in 1806 and opened a level in 1809 on the Dinas Uchaf Estate. To gain access to the Glamorganshire Canal he completed a tramroad in 1810 to link with Dr Richard Griffiths's tramroad at Gyfeillon. Coffin sank the first shaft in the Rhondda Valley on Graig-ddu land at Dinas in 1812 and extracted bituminous coal at a depth of 40 yards from the Rhondda No 3 Seam. The seam, which became known as 'Coffin's Coal', was a good quality house-coal and excellent for use by blacksmiths and for providing coke for industry.

In 1832 Coffin sank another shaft—the Dinas Middle Colliery—to reach the No 3 Seam at a depth of 80 yards and by 1841 employed 301 men and 113 boys at his Dinas pits and levels. He lived at Llandaff and was often to be seen riding in a coal tram to and from Dinas for part of his journey. He became a director of the Taff Vale Railway in 1841. He opened pits at Trealaw in 1839 and at Tonypandy in 1845. In 1852 he became MP for Cardiff and spent his last years in London where he died in 1867 aged 82.

In the early Dinas pits and those at Pontypridd, coal was hauled to the surface by a hempen rope wound round a whim or kind of windlass turned by a horse walking round in a circle. Hempen ropes were replaced eventually by iron-link chains made at Brown Lenox chain-works. Later, some pits used water-balance headgear for winding men and coal and 60 such devices were in use in Glamorgan collieries in 1861. An iron water-storage tank of about two tons capacity on the platform at the top of the shaft was filled to a point at which its weight, and that of an empty tram resting on it, was greater than the weight of a full tram of coal on an empty tank waiting at the bottom of the shaft. The descending tank with its greater weight brought the full tram of coal to the surface. The water below was pumped to the surface and the procedure continued. Miners going up and down the shaft clung in a precarious cluster on the water tank. Water-balances gave way to steam-powered winding engines in the pits of Pontypridd and throughout the South Wales coalfield.

The increasing demand for steam coal after 1840 was chiefly responsible for the development of mining in Pontypridd, the Rhondda and elsewhere. Sinking deep to the steam coal measures was risky and much of the early exploration was ventured upon by the Marquess of Bute's Trustees who owned extensive areas of land in the valleys. The Bute Dock had opened in Cardiff in 1839 and sought increased trade. Just before Christmas 1855—four years after the first sinkings—the pioneer train of Rhondda steam coal passed through Pontypridd on its way to the docks. Sinkings increased in the early 1870s and 23 new collieries opened in the Rhondda between 1872 and 1882, greatly increasing the number of long coal trains trundling through Pontypridd. Annual coal output in South Wales rose from about eight million tons in 1857 to 17 million tons in 1877 and to 35 million tons in 1897.

Early miners carried candles to give light at the coal face. Safety lamps, although not compulsory even in the 1870s, were increasingly used after 1840 when explosions in local pits sternly emphasised the dangers of working with naked lights in fiery seams and in poorly ventilated pits. One early method of providing pit ventilation was the use of a coal-fired furnace situated in the underground roadway leading to the upcast shaft. Air in the mine became heated as it passed over the furnace and rose in the shaft to create a draught throughout the mine. A current of fresh, cold air entered the pit at the downcast shaft or through a partitioned section of a single-shaft mine.

The dangers of this method of ventilation grew as pits were sunk deeper. The release of firedamp or highly inflammable methane gas from the steam-coal seams led to its ignition followed by an explosion. Mining engineers were slow to realise that coal dust ignited by firedamp could flash-flame throughout a mine workings. It would be followed by a discharge of afterdamp, a mainly carbon dioxide gas, and a small explosion could be transformed into a sudden catastrophe. Twelve men died in an explosion at Dinas in 1844, 114 in 1856 at Cymmer (Porth), 178 in 1867 at Ferndale and another 53 there in 1869, 268 at Abercarn in 1878, 63 at Dinas in 1879, 101 at Penygraig in 1880, 119 at Risca also in 1880, and 81 at Maerdy in 1885. There were many more major disasters and in 1894 an explosion at the Albion

Colliery at Cilfynydd caused the greatest single mining tragedy in Wales to that time when 290 miners were killed.

At Cilfynydd, sinking of the Albion began in December 1884 on the site of Ynyscaedudwg Farm, with two shafts 33 yards apart, 19ft in diameter and lined with brick. In March 1886 part of one shaft collapsed and two men were killed by falling clay and bricks. In November the same year one of the shafts had reached a depth of 600ft and was partly brick-lined. William Jones was below supervising some pumping operations and the work of fourteen or more sinkers when several yards of lining collapsed and tons of bricks fell down the shaft, killing four men instantly. Some sinkers were engulfed in the debris while others crouched for protection on one side of the shaft. Groans were heard and, although exposed to danger from more falling bricks, the survivors shovelled frantically in the dust-filled gloom and tore at the debris with their hands. One man was trapped by a girder across his body. Water started to rise in the shaft and quickly reached the man's chin, threatening to drown him before he could be released. One rescuer baled water from the man's mouth with a leather cap; one shielded him from more falling bricks; while other men levered at the girder with crowbars. Their butty was freed and brought to the surface and into the sunshine thanks to the brave rescue.

Many miners were killed or seriously injured in single accidents in local pits throughout the Victorian period and later. They died in roof falls or were crushed by journeys of trams or fell from winding cages. There were scores of small-scale tragedies: five men were burnt in a explosion in the Hetty Pit in August 1900, and the *Pontypridd Observer* and other newspapers told of many accidents to miners. Sinking of the Albion continued and the first coal came to the surface in August 1887. Eight large 'districts' were opened up in the years approaching the fateful month of June 1894 for the Albion.

Coalfield Unrest

Coalowners reduced wages by 15 per cent in 1857 and several thousand miners in Pontypridd and the Rhondda called a strike. Hordes of black-legs stormed into Pontypridd by train and descended on local collieries. Troops were called in to maintain order. The strike was quickly broken and hungry miners were forced to accept the coalowners' terms. Miners failed to grasp the advantage of their strong bargaining position in the mid-1860s. Coalowners still claimed that wage reductions were necessary to compensate for falling coal prices but their greater concern was to avoid stoppages of work. They now had to recover not only variable costs such as wages but some of the fixed costs of deep mining to extract steam coal which were not incurred in working shallow pits and levels. Pit ventilation, haulage, winding, and the cutting and maintenance of long underground roadways was expensive and required large capital investment.

The coalowners decided in January 1868 to reduce the wages by another 15 per cent and to introduce cheaper working methods. On 1 May Pontypridd miners joined the long strike by most of the pits in Monmouthshire and were supported by miners from twenty Rhondda pits. But the strike collapsed within two weeks and the wage reductions had to be accepted. The ice and fire of unionist attitudes among miners surged and receded through the Victorian years. Miners did not want a centralised union but preferred their own district unions. Many of these were split into small, independent units and these divisions prevented any hope of unity in the coalfield. Many miners could not afford to pay union dues from the low wages they took home. A collier, or hewer, earned about 20s a week from 1841 to 1888 with dips and rises from time to time. Miners in the early years had money deducted from their pay for candles and tools supplied. From 1889 to 1891, when coal prices were high, wages ranged from 24s to 29s but were down again to 23s and less from 1892 to 1898. They stood at 25s a week in 1899 and 33s in 1900.

The first 'Sliding Scale' agreement on wages was signed in December 1875 and, with revisions, lasted in South Wales for 25 years. The agreement meant that as the average selling price of coal rose and fell the miners' wages fluctuated accordingly. Securing the men's compliance with its terms gave the coalowners a big stick which generally subdued any ideas about strike action and supported an incentive for the owners to sell coal more cheaply from increased production. It also refuted the most important argument for unionism among miners by making the issue of collective bargaining on pay and conditions redundant.

A joint committee of owners and miners supervised the operation of the sliding scale agreement, guarding their individual interests. The creator of the agreement and the first chairman of the committee was

Sir William Thomas Lewis, later Lord Merthyr, who acted for the coalowners. The vice-chairman throughout the life of the committee from 1875 to 1903, elected after a ballot of miners, was William Abraham, better known by his Bardic name 'Mabon', who favoured the sliding scale for many years and advocated the formation of local unions. He was zealously opposed by William Brace who considered the working of the agreement impractical. A fall in wages between November 1891 and June 1893, aggravated by a rise in the cost of living, inflamed unrest among miners and fanned the smouldering campaign to throw out the agreement. James Keir Hardie, who edited the weekly *Labour Leader* newspaper, wrote in 1895 that under the sliding scale the conditions of the miners had gone from bad to worse while trade unionism had become virtually extinct.

Rocking Stone Strike

By the summer of 1893 hauliers, who earned only about 18s a week, sought a 20 per cent increase in wages and came out on strike. The dispute started on 1 August among hauliers in the Ogmore Valley and was spread rapidly by 'marching gangs' of men. They succeeded in bringing out 40,000 men in South Wales while 90,000 more were threatened with lock-outs. The dispute caused deep conflict between two rival unions. The Cambrian Miners' Association, led by Mabon who condemned the strike as illegal and dishonourable, faced the Miners' Federation of Great Britain (MFGB) led by William Brace, who supported the strike.

Pontypridd lay in the centre of the strike area and mass meetings were held in August at the Rocking Stone on the Common, which led to the dispute being called the 'Rocking Stone Strike'. On 11 August 10,000 miners attended a meeting there. They first assembled at the Tumble in town and, headed by brass bands, marched with their colourful banners through the town to the Common. The eloquent Morgan Thomas, a haulier from Pentre, addressed the meeting. He stood on the Rocking Stone and his firebrand oratory kindled the assembly to denounce the sliding scale, to support the demand for better wages and to call for unity in the coalfield. But the majority of miners in Glamorgan rejected the strikers and later took over the hauliers' duties.

Above: The Albion Colliery, Cilfynydd, now the site of the Coed-y-Lan Comprehensive School. Sinking of the Albion on Ynyscaedudwg Fields began in 1884. 290 miners died in an explosion at the colliery on 23 June 1894, the greatest single mining tragedy in Wales until the nearby Senghenydd explosion in 1913. **Below:** Headgear and stack of the Albion Colliery, 1957.

Above: Maritime Colliery at Maesycoed, Pontypridd. **Below:** Great Western Collieries, near Hopkinstown, Pontypridd.

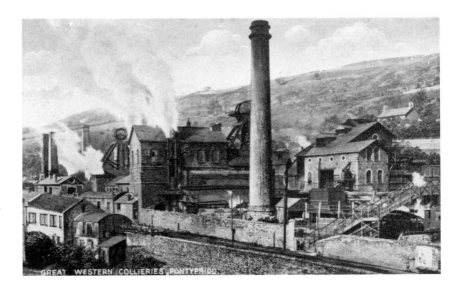

Above: Cwm Cottage, site of the Cwm Colliery. **Below:** Workmen's Hall, Cilfynydd, in 1957. Built in 1894, the year of the Albion Colliery disaster. Recently demolished and replaced by a new community centre on the site.

Above: Mabon unveiling a monument at Llanfabon in 1907 to eleven victims of the Albion disaster. **Below:** Workers at Lewis Merthyr colliery, *c.* 1900.

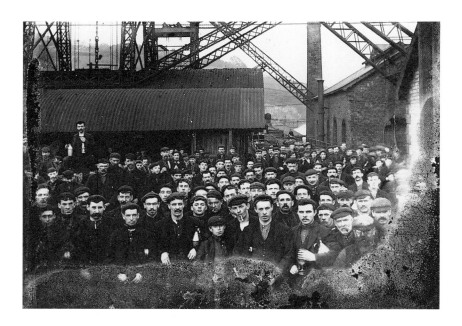

Above: High Street, showing the City Restaurant, centre, the Empire Music Hall entrance, left, and the Royal Clarence Theatre on the right, *c.* 1899. **Below:** Pontypridd Markets Co. buildings in Market Street, decorated for the 1935 Silver Jubilee.

Coalowners set up an emergency committee and, in a claim of 'justified protection for the loyal workers', obtained agreement for extra police to be drafted to the area. Special constables were sworn in, for the colliery managers feared serious breaches of the peace which were threatened by strikers and non-strikers who taunted each other at the pitheads in Pontypridd, the Rhondda and elsewhere. The committee sent off telegrams asking for troops to be brought in to quell the disturbances and at one time there were 2,000 soldiers in South Wales. The marching gangs were dispersed. A throng of 20,000 miners assembled at the Rocking Stone on 2 September. They passed several resolutions, including a call for the resignation of the miners' representatives on the joint committee. But hunger was more resolute. The hauliers surrendered and full working was resumed at the pits by 11 September. The MFGB supporters had not dented the fortress walls of the sliding scale agreement, but their battle led to the formation five years later of the South Wales Miners' Federation.

Albion Disaster

Church bells rang out joyously in London on Saturday 23 June 1894. Thousands waving Union flags cheered and danced their way lightly through the sunlit streets. Queen Victoria had been presented with a new great-grandson, the future Prince of Wales, who in 1936 as King Edward VIII would abdicate the throne and become Duke of Windsor. In the streets of Cilfynydd that grey afternoon, the wail of pit hooters summoned hundreds of miners to the pithead. Clutching their water-jacks and tommy-boxes of sandwiches the men strode from the hillside terraces of the village down to the Albion Colliery, their heavy boots ringing on pavement and crunching on road. Other miners walked along the canal bank from Pontypridd, Trallwn, Coedpenmaen, Pontshon-norton and Abercynon. That day they died. And nearly 150 wives joined the queen in widowhood. More than 330 children lost their fathers. Thousands of local people were united in grief for their lost sons and brothers and sweethearts and friends.

From his shop window in Richard Street, Cilfynydd, watchmaker John Hopkins peered over his glasses at the afternoon shoppers taking their baskets to the many food shops in the street. He had seen the dust-blackened faces of many of the thousand miners of the day shift go home. He watched many of the 300 men of the 'night' shift (who worked from 2 till 8 p.m.) go to the pit. As the seconds ticked by to ten minutes to four, draper Stephen Evans was attending to two ladies who wanted to buy some cloth and he picked up his scissors to cut a length of material from the newly arrived roll of black dress-material, which would soon be wanted by teams of dressmakers working day and night to make mourning black. At his surgery at 'Dundella', beside the Workmen's Hall built that year for the Albion miners, Dr James Shaw Lyttle was working in his dispensary when he heard a loud explosion quickly followed by another. He looked through a window towards the Albion Colliery and saw clouds of dust and smoke spread over the wooden headgear of the upcast and downcast shafts and rise high above the sheaves. He hurried to the pithead, joining the streams of men and women running fearfully to the scene from all parts of the village.

Miners working on the surface near the shafts were blown over by the blasts and blinded by the rising coal dust. Some felt the heat of the explosion and had their eyebrows singed. The blasts blew away part of the staging round the downcast shaft and dislodged the wooden covering over the Schiele ventilation fan. The colliery manager Phillip Jones, his son William, James Groves, William Garnett and other miners went down the shaft within an hour to investigate. Timbers were burning at the pit bottom and along the heading or roadway to the lamp station at Dudson's Heading on the Grover's side of the pit where the men found many mutilated and badly burned bodies.

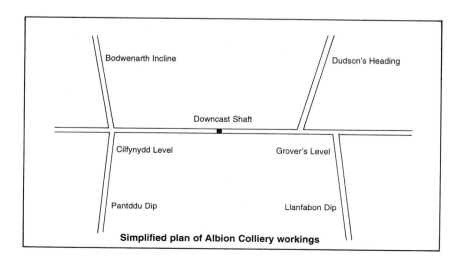

Simplified plan of Albion Colliery workings

Bodwenarth Incline

Dudson's Heading

Downcast Shaft

Cilfynydd Level

Grover's Level

Pantddu Dip

Llanfabon Dip

The search party returned to the surface after two hours and brought out two injured men. But both men died shortly afterwards. The sight of survivors gave hope to anxious relatives and friends gathered at the pithead, especially when one rescuer, J.P. Gibbon, came to the surface carrying a young boy on his back. The boy was William Henry Dobbs whose father, fireman William Dobbs, died in the explosion. The boy said that he was in a manhole, a recess cut in the side of the roadway, near the bottom of the shaft when the explosion blew a man named Jenkins into the manhole with him. When the dust subsided they made for the shaft and Jenkins told the boy to hang on to the tail of his coat and follow him in the blackness between the burning roof-support frames. Jenkins became exhausted and could go no further. He told the boy to go on alone, and then died. Dobbs neared the shaft but a roof fall blocked his way. He clawed at the debris until he saw the light carried by his rescuer.

The first of the dead miners was brought to the surface by 9.15 p.m. and then more and more badly mutilated bodies imprinted grim evidence that the explosion was more serious than first believed. Growing numbers of victims were carried on stretchers made from brattice cloth to a long building near the downcast shaft used as stables for pit horses. The dead miners were laid in long rows in the hayloft overhead and covered with blankets and sacks. From the wooden stairway to the hayloft, policemen shepherded lines of distraught relatives who searched by the light of lanterns looking for their loved ones. Some bodies were wrongly identified and had to be returned to the hayloft the next day from homes in the village. Councillor W.H. Gronow of Pleasant View, Cilfynydd, identified the bodies of his three sons, William, Richard and Evan.

Before midnight, J.T. Robson, HM Inspector of Mines, and two assistant inspectors went down the pit where Phillip Jones, William Lewis, the Albion Colliery agent, and search parties awaited them. By 3 a.m. they had reached the double parting along the Grover's Level where the roadway divided at Dudson's Heading. They branched down Llanfabon Dip a little further along until roof falls blocked their way. They found the body of Richard Owen, a young Pontshonnorton man known as 'Mabon Bach'. The force of the explosion had blown off a leg and had decapitated him. Bodies of torn and burnt men were found in most parts of the pit. More than 30 were found in workings at the end of Dudson's Heading. They had died from suffocation from afterdamp gas. More were found suffocated by the gas in Pantddu Dip on the Cilfynydd side of the pit.

Griffith Bunford (reported in 1894 as George Bumford) survived. He was cutting timber with other men at Mordecai's level in Pantddu Dip, which was one of the wettest parts of the pit. He mopped his forehead and passed an axe to his butty, Hugh Pugh, and stood back as the explosions echoed through the roadways. The men wondered whether to make for the shaft or try to find shelter from the fire expected in a moment. The pit doors crashed open and a wind seared through the level, bringing a blinding and choking fine coal dust which put their safety lamps out. A swirl of heated air passed over them but did not burn them. The men lurched along Pantddu Dip and saw a weird blue light—caused by the highly inflammable firedamp near the roof—which lit the darkness with its notorious 'flame of the blue devils'. The men hastened along the Dip before the deadly afterdamp would arrive to kill them. Hugh Pugh suffocated but Bunford scrambled on until he, too, faltered but was found by a rescue party. He lived until he was aged over 80. The explosion had passed along every main road of the mine except Pantddu Dip and the mine inspectors considered that the wetness of the Dip and the general absence of coal dust there had stopped the explosion from wreaking havoc in this area.

Thomas Howells also survived. He was working in Curly's level in the Bodwenarth Incline when his lamp went out. He, too, saw the eerie blue light and made his way to the lamp station where the Incline met Pantddu Dip on the Cilfynydd Level. He choked and collapsed but was found in time and revived. Two other miners, David Lewis and George Martin, were also brought out of the pit alive. They survived.

New searches were made throughout the pit on Sunday morning and by noon another hundred bodies had been recovered and carried to the hayloft. About 20,000 sightseers had flocked to the Albion Colliery by the afternoon and the police had difficulty stopping them from crossing the little humpbacked bridge which stepped over the canal and led to the colliery. They allowed only immediate relatives through to the pithead and extra police were hurriedly drafted in from Merthyr and Cardiff to control the crowds. Religious leaders condemned the irredeemable persons who sent drays of beer for the sightseers to consume on a Sunday and so prolonged the stay of the curious.

Herbert Asquith, the Home Secretary, sent a message of sympathy to the bereaved families on behalf of Queen Victoria. In Parliament,

William Abraham MP (Mabon) got up to interrupt the announcement of the birth of Prince Edward and said, 'One moment, please. Before we express joy at the great news let us express our sympathy with the stricken families of Cilfynydd'. The House stood in sympathy.

Throughout the harrowing days, crowds of relatives waited at the pithead in despair as rescue parties searched through the pit, hampered by the heavy falls of roof. Several bodies were recovered up to two weeks after the explosion. The final death toll in the Albion explosion was 290. There was no reliable list of men at work in the pit at the time of the explosion and the police posted notices in the local villages asking if anyone was missing.

An open-air service was conducted at Cilfynydd on Tuesday 27 June and several funerals took place at Glyntaff Cemetery. The first of the mass funerals took place the following day. Thousands of mourners gathered on Cilfynydd Common near the colliery. Eight coffins left for Llanfabon churchyard and new bearers took over frequently along the route. A cortège of 41 bodies, the coffins placed on horse-drawn biers and accompanied by hundreds of silent mourners, trailed from Cilfynydd along Merthyr Road to Glyntaff. On Thursday morning, 53 more miners were buried at Glyntaff and other coffins left Cilfynydd for Pontypridd railway station to be taken for burial in the Rhondda and other parts of Wales. The bodies of eleven miners who had not been identified were buried at Llanfabon. The miners leader Mabon unveiled a monument to them at Llanfabon churchyard in July 1907.

Of the 120 horses working underground at the time of the Albion explosion, 118 were killed. The carcasses were buried behind Mary Street in the widely spreading lower spoil heap which by 1900 had reached up to the rock cliff-face of the mountain.

It emerged from the inquest held in Pontypridd in July that unwanted timbers underground which could not be hewed out quickly or easily were drilled and the holes packed with about two ounces of dynamite. This was fired by a fuse lit by a spill of paper, itself ignited by placing it against the gauze of the Clanny safety lamps used by miners at the pit. The manager, Phillip Jones, insisted that shot-firing took place only between shifts. The question arose as to how blasting could take place between shifts when the night shift arrived at the mine at 2 p.m. as the day shift left the mine. Survivors of the explosion confirmed that blasting did take place during the Saturday night shift.

The Inspector of Mines gave his opinion that the evidence indicated that shots were fired in the timbers in several levels and roadways, that the holes drilled in the timbers for the dynamite were not properly 'tamped' with rubble, and that the shots were fired by the night overman or the night fireman and were not set off by the explosion itself. Also, that watering in the fiery, dry and dusty mine was not adequate to keep the coal dust down.

Many mining experts considered that evidence had proved that the highly inflammable firedamp was not itself the major cause of pit explosions but that certain combinations of coal dust and air caused the explosions. Inspector Henry Hall considered that at Cilfynydd the blasting of the timbers had ignited an accumulation of gas in the roof. The burning gas had ignited the coal dust and 'knock-on-effect' explosions had travelled through the mine. Court proceedings were taken against several Albion Colliery officials under the rules of the 1887 Mines Regulation Act. The charges were dismissed, withdrawn or not proven. The Albion was soon back to the production of nearly 45,000 tons of coal a month.

The Albion Colliery was closed in 1966. The two shafts were capped and the buildings demolished. The Coed-y-Lan Comprehensive School and its playing fields now occupy the site. The Albion spoil tip which towered over Cilfynydd was more widely spread out in the 1970s to improve stability (although its presence still causes the villagers concern) following representations by the villagers after the 1966 disaster at the not-too-distant village of Aberfan, where a spoil tip collapsed and slurry surged down the mountainside to engulf 116 children and 28 adults who died when the school was buried.

Part of the Albion tip was spread over an area of the Eglwysilan mountain and covered an ancient tumulus known as Twyn-yr-Arian, called locally 'the money tump', which was a favourite walk and meeting place for the Victorian miners of the Albion. Some believed that the tumulus, on a rise near the two grey cairns which still remain, was the burial place of an ancient Welsh chieftain. The Albion miners met here with the men of Senghenydd, close below in the Rhymney Valley, who would know their own, even greater disaster in 1913 when 439 men died in a devastating underground explosion at their colliery.

Bread, Banners and Bayonets

In 1897 miners and their families found it difficult to live on an average weekly wage which plummeted from 23s to 20s 10d. Coal-owners wanted to reduce production costs while miners wanted to improve their lot. The owners refused to listen to pleas for minimum wage guarantees and miners determined that any improved agreements would only be achieved by strike action. Miners held a ballot, gave the coalowners six months notice from 1 October 1897 to end the sliding scale and demanded a 10 per cent wage increase. The owners retaliated by declaring a lock-out from 1 April 1898 when miners would get one month's notice.

Mabon, the miners' leader, a strong supporter of the sliding scale, was now convinced that changes to the current agreement were essential. Mabon (1842–1920) had worked as a door-boy in his local colliery at Cwmavon when he was ten years old. He moved to the Rhondda in 1877 and became agent of the local miners' union. He was elected Liberal MP for the Rhondda in 1885 and held his seat through seven successive general elections. In 1888 he won for his men a holiday (Mabon's Day) on the first Monday of every month. It was intended to combat over-production at the pits, which led to a reduction in prices and cuts in wages. Mabon and his opponent William Brace were generally reconciled, but Mabon warned that in any long conflict the spectre of starvation would force miners back to work on terms dictated by the coalowners. Strike funds were low, for many miners with little interest in unionism still refused to pay any union dues. At a meeting at the White Hart in Pontypridd in October 1897 miners resolved that all men should join the Hauliers' Union and support the proposed strike to start in April 1898.

The strike began. After a ballot, the miners' representatives on the sliding scale joint committee failed to gain absolute powers to act for the men and the coalowners no longer recognised them. Mabon urged negotiation and for the men to return to work 'if the employers would allow them to do so'. Political journalist Keir Hardie—later the founder of the Labour Party—attacked the remark as being an encouragement for the owners to prolong the struggle. At a conference for delegates representing 10,000 men, Mabon failed to gain the chairmanship: instead, the voters elected John Williams of Ynysybwl who had been a checkweigher at the Lady Windsor Colliery and later became an MP.

The miners were prepared to go back down the pits for a 10 per cent pay rise but the owners threw out the proposal.

Miners and their families soon knew hunger and soup kitchens were set up throughout Pontypridd. John Evans of the Commercial Hotel in Cilfynydd lent a number of cooking stoves, and 1,000 men, women and children were fed daily at a relief station in Coedpenmaen. The Maypole Dairy in Taff Street was the first local grocer to give relief supplies for free meals to be prepared in the vestry of Penuel Chapel. Many helpers arranged breakfasts for children. Employees of Hopkin Morgan bakeries in Trallwn collected 50s every week for the local relief fund. Dr HamlenWilliams of 'Fairfield' in Hawthorn distributed 1,000lb of beef and a ton of potatoes in early May. He personally employed 30 strikers every day to trim hedges and tidy the area. A new gang of men took their places every three days to earn vital shillings.

In mid-May, another miners' delegates conference elected Mabon as chairman. Resolutions from many pits gave the delegates powers to negotiate a settlement of the strike which was already causing distress. Miners met in late May at the Empire Music Hall in Pontypridd and pointed out that the extra money pocketed by the coalowners from reduced railway charges would easily pay for the 10 per cent increase wanted. But on 31 May the owners refused to concede the increase and rejected demands that a conciliation board should replace the sliding scale agreement. They refused to consider reopening the pits before a permanent settlement was reached. Mabon's Day must be abolished and the 'character note', or discharge reference system without which a miner could not get another job in the coalfield, must stay.

Pontypridd shopkeepers continued to give food to miners and their families as the strike entered June 1898. Hodges of Market Street gave breakfasts for 750 children. For over six weeks, the solicitors Spickett & Son and Thomas Jones of Glen View brewery on the Graig gave breakfasts alternately for Graig children, and breakfasts for children throughout the Pontypridd district were arranged by Miss Spickett of Bronwydd House. Meals were also provided by William Pegler the grocer, clerks of the London and National Provincial Bank, and quarrymen at Graig-yr-Hesg and Darenddu. At Cilfynydd, wives of the Albion Colliery officials ensured that children attending schools in Cilfynydd and Pontshonnorton had tea and some bread and butter before going into the classrooms. The Town Ward Relief Committee had provided 25,000 breakfasts and teas by mid-June. The urban

district council opened a stone-breaking yard in a quarry on the
Common and alternate gangs of men broke up stones for use in
roadway improvements and earned a few shillings for food. Cadbury's
sent a case of cocoa for distribution among Graig families. Publicans
made collections of pennies to buy bread and boots for children.

Pawnbroker Otto Faller in Taff Street was inundated with depositors and handed out innumerable half-crowns for goods pledged over
the long months of the strike. Samuel Evans the MP for Mid Glamorgan told that the wives of many miners 'had sold every household
item possible to the pawnbrokers—first the pictures and the ornaments;
then the furniture even to the bedstead and the bedding; the plates and
dishes and cups went one or two at a time for a few pence with which
to buy bread; and even clothes and boots were pawned until a glance
into the miners' houses showed nothing but the bare walls. If the rent
had not been paid, the bailiffs were sent to the houses to distrain on
goods or evict the families'.

Troops were drafted into South Wales and created ill-feeling
throughout the coalfield. Cavalry of the 6th Dragoon Guards arrived in
Pontypridd in the early hours of Sunday 12 June. The officers were
billeted at the New Inn Hotel and the men at the Lesser Town Hall and
in tents pitched in farm fields adjoining Maesycoed House. A troop of
50 men turned out on Monday morning and trotted their horses down
the Broadway in a colourful threat of strength. Interested and curious
spectators and groups of miners with their bright display of banners
watched the manoeuvres at Taff Vale Park, which included sword-
slicing of lemons fixed to poles.

Sir Alfred Thomas MP asked the Home Secretary to consider
whether troops should be withdrawn from districts where disturbances
had not yet occurred. He was referred to the local authorities which had
requested the troops in the belief that the police would not be able to
contain the disorder. A Swansea MP asked the Home Secretary if he
was aware that the Pontypridd stipendiary magistrate had received a
letter from local magistrates commanding him to instruct the troops in
the area, if it became necessary, to charge a crowd, use bayonets and
open fire with ball cartridges. Were the officers in command of the
troops bound to obey these instructions? The Home Secretary said that
he knew of no such letter but the law required that an officer, when
called upon by a magistrate to take action, had absolute discretion as
to what action should be taken, the arms to be used and the point when

firing became necessary.

On Wednesday 22 June, a squadron of cavalry based at Pontypridd was sent to control disturbances at Merthyr. When the Chief Constable, Captain Lindsay, asked that the rest be sent to Dowlais, the stipendiary magistrate refused as this action would leave Pontypridd unprotected. Keir Hardie reported in his *Labour Leader* that in Pontypridd a special train with steam up was ready to convey soldiers to trouble-spots. He addressed a mass meeting of strikers and supporters on 28 June at the Rocking Stone. Some days earlier, soldiers stationed at Mountain Ash had become drunk and had created a disturbance in the village streets. Women were insulted and fights broke out between soldiers and local miners. The *Pontypridd Observer* called for police reinforcements to keep the soldiers in check and said that local magistrates should dash off telegrams for more troops to be sent to Pontypridd to keep those already here in order.

Coalowners and miners hardened their attitudes over the long, hot and sultry weeks. Troops passed the time by scooping up the manure their parading horses had deposited thickly along the Broadway; and by entertaining thousands of spectators with tournaments held in the Maritime Colliery field. In just over a year, all the cavalrymen stationed in Pontypridd were serving in the Boer War in South Africa.

Reluctantly, miners at many collieries in South Wales passed a resolution in August 1898 to accept the sliding scale agreement if it would guarantee a minimum wage rate. The coalowners at first refused to negotiate. But they had suffered heavy losses during the long strike and eventually agreed to include in an agreement a clause that, miners' leaders persuaded a delegate conference in Cardiff on 31 August, guaranteed in effect a minimum wage. The miners had suffered five months of hardship and hunger. They accepted the coalowners' terms and the sliding scale. Mabon's Day was abolished. The agreement was signed on 1 September 1898 and pit hooters sounded the end of the strike.

The South Wales Miners' Federation was formally established on 11 October 1898. Mabon was elected president and William Brace vice-president. The federation became strong and in May 1899 its membership stood at 92,000, increasing to 104,000 by the end of the year. Not all miners wanted to join and in the early years of its life the union served notice to end contracts at many pits to compel miners to join. Over the next five years, nearly 70 stoppages of work took place on the old, tempestuous question of unionism. Pontypridd branch members often had fiery meetings at the Green Meadow Hotel on the Graig. Miners still held mass meetings at the Rocking Stone on the Common and on 23 July 1900 Mabon and three other MPs addressed more than 10,000 men assembled there who resolved with a great show of hands to demand yet again a fixed minimum wage.

In March 1903 a conciliation board, upholding the principle of a minimum wage, was established and the controversial sliding scale came to an end. In July 1909 the miners' Eight Hour Day Act came into force. William 'Mabon' Abraham and William Brace finally worked together in the new trade union for the miners of the South Wales coalfield.

Chapter 8

On the Town

'Oyez, Oyez!', town crier and bill-poster James Thyer boomed as he rang his bell at the junction of Taff Street and Mill Street one day in March 1897. His rousing calls had commanded attention in the town for several years as had those of Frederick Thompson who was the town crier in 1879. 'Thyer the Crier' cleared his throat: 'Lord John Sangster's mammoth and celebrated circus is coming to Pontypridd. It will be held at the People's Park in Millfield on Wednesday the seventh of April and will stay for the Easter holiday. This particular show is dedicated to Her Majesty Queen Victoria's forthcoming Diamond Jubilee. Oyez, Oyez!'

The circus parade of bands, clowns, jugglers and other performers, carriages and wagons, chariots drawn by plumed horses with jingling harness, elephants draped with gold and red and blue silks and velvets, and showmen's traction engines hauling a procession of caged lions and tigers and apes left the Bridge Street end of town one morning and stretched for two miles along Taff Street and the Broadway. A mass of spectators packed the pavements to watch the great show go by. Later at Millfield 5,000 people were seated in a two-pole tent. The arena was gaily decorated with flags and bunting and glittering silver tinsel, carpeted with sand and sawdust and brilliantly lit by electricity (generated by dynamos driven by traction engines), and flaring naphtha torches.

The Victorians of Pontypridd loved circuses and fairs. Amusements set up in Captain Williams's field (the old Fairfield and now the car park opposite the YMCA in Taff Street) and also in the yard of the Butchers Arms drew a crush of fun seekers to their switchbacks, carousels and shooting galleries. The main streets would be thronged on these occasions with itinerant traders, merchants, acrobats and jugglers. The din would go on until late at night and everyone enjoyed fish and chips, fist fights and faggots and peas. The Victorians loved celebrations, too, and grasped every opportunity for festivity to escape momentarily from the severity of everyday life. There was great discussion as to whether the twentieth century actually began on 1 January

1900 or 1901. The Victorians did not mind and went on the town for an extra special New Year's Eve in both years just to make sure.

Jubilee

To celebrate Queen Victoria's Diamond Jubilee in 1897, Sir Alfred Thomas MP entertained 20,000 children of East Glamorgan. In May and June he presented each of them with a jubilee medal and provided teas in their schools and on Pontypridd Common. The Jubilee Cake baked by Hopkin Morgan weighed a total of five tons. The 261 inmates of the Graig Workhouse and those of the Cottage Homes at Church Village sat down to a special dinner that had the air of a banquet. The town was profusely decked out with red, white and blue bunting and flags and displays. An arch built over the entrance to Brown Lenox chainworks was surmounted with a ship's wheel, laurelled anchors and a giant leek. Pontypridd Gaslight Co. festooned the archway of the Old Bridge with hundreds of small coloured lights which floated their reflections in the river. The Fountain and the front of the Conservative Club opposite were wreathed with chains of multicoloured gas lamps.

A huge bonfire blazed on Eglwysilan mountain and fireworks were let off on the Common at sunset to light the crags with roman candles and showers of golden rain. Rockets soared from the roof of the Royal Clarence Theatre and burst into rainbow-coloured stars to cries of delight and admiration from the merrymakers in Taff Street which was stringed from end to end with candle lanterns. Jubilee sports were held at Taff Vale Park in June with foot-races, bicycle handicaps and carnivals. The field was lined with scores of tradesmen's horse and spring-carts competing for prizes for the best turned out and decorated entrants.

Entertainment

The Royal Clarence Theatre adjoined the Clarence Hotel in Pontypridd High Street and was built in the early 1890s. It was the first permanent theatre built in the South Wales coalfield and could seat an audience of a thousand. It was renamed the New Theatre when extended in 1901, and after further extensions and alterations in 1938 became the County

Cinema. The Royal Clarence was built by John Trenchard and cared for later by his son, Charles. The theatre was lit throughout by electricity but with emergency gaslight. Smoking was banned.

A Town Hall, situated at Pontypridd Market, was built in 1885 for £1,600 and seated 700. It was replaced in importance in 1890 by the New Town Hall with a seating capacity of 1,700. The smaller hall (now the Clothes Market hall) was known as the Lesser Hall from 1899 and the new hall was known simply as the Town Hall. But although a licence was obtained for theatrical performances by the Lesser Hall, the new Town Hall failed to secure such a licence until after the Victorian era. Dr Joseph Parry, of the South Wales School of Music in Cardiff, gave a lecture concert at the new hall in 1899 on the subject 'The Great Masters of Music' with musical illustrations. General Booth of the Salvation Army preached there in 1900 and Winston Churchill held a political meeting there in 1905.

Dancing was very popular in Victorian Pontypridd, the favourite dances being the waltz, the polka and the barn dance. Men smartly dressed in suits and in shirts with stiffly starched three-inch high collars escorted their ladies who wore long silk, satin, brocade or velvet dresses with accordion-pleated sun-ray or yoke skirts which fitted tightly at the hips and flared out to the dance floor. Bodices were usually low in front and square-cut or V-shaped. In the late 1890s it was fashionable for ladies to wear their hair brushed to a bun, or in a 'teapot handle' style having a hanging loop from a coil high at the back of the head. Dances were held regularly at the County, New Inn and Park hotels which all had chandeliers illuminated by gaslight and electric lamps.

Town Pubs

There were over a hundred pubs in Victorian Pontypridd (listed in the Appendix) and many no longer exist. Some were demolished to allow for modern developments, such as the Llanbradach Arms near the Machine Bridge at Treforest, which now lies under a slip road to the A470. Others fell victim to the rise of clubs or the pressures of modern-day economics. A number became business premises, including the Danygraig Arms on the Broadway, where today the famous 'Grogg' sculptures are created at John Hughes's Welsh Crafts Pottery. Some pubs passed away from sheer old age or were pensioned off into houses or flats. And those that were simple beerhouses, where beer was served in the parlour, have reverted to private homes. Others were rebuilt or altered, and changed their names, such as the Bunch of Grapes in the High Street at the Tumble which became the Criterion in 1904.

In late Victorian years, when beer cost 2d or 3d a pint, a sovereign could buy a round of about 100 pints. But the weekly wage of a postman, for example, was under a pound. Local miners, railwaymen and heavy manual workers might earn 30s to 40s or more. Many service and other workers earned substantially less. Drunk and disorderly behaviour resulted in fines of 5s or 10s for the offenders. Or perhaps a £1 or a week in Cardiff Gaol. For many on their last legs it was up the road to the Graig Workhouse. Drinking on a Sunday in Wales was against the law from 1882 but some licensees risked their livelihoods by leaving the back door on the latch. The police could easily smell them out.

The New Inn, a farmhouse in the 1730s, later became a famous hotel. It was demolished in 1982 but is well remembered for its many bars, dining and coffee rooms, billiards room, dance hall and magnificent wide staircase of 1922. The original early eighteenth-century inn was a much smaller building fronted with trees. The New Inn was a commercial and family hotel with a large stables and yard; it was also a post house where horses could be changed for long-distance travellers. The Petty Sessions for the Upper Division of Miskin were held there until the 1860s, when the court transferred from the White Hart Hotel. John George Cousins was landlord at this time. The New Inn was rebuilt in 1893 and Mrs Elizabeth Miles was landlady through the late Victorian years.

Further up Taff Street at today's shopping precinct was the now demolished Tredegar Arms, kept in 1850 by Thomas Williams. It stood on the corner of Turnpike Lane which led down to a small cattle market that was extended in 1909. On the opposite corner was Crosswell's off-licence and wine shop, the site of a toll-house from where turnpike gates once stretched across Taff Street. From the 1860s the landlord of the Tredegar Arms was Thomas Evans followed by John Evans, a farrier or shoesmith who had a small forge behind the pub. The tinkle and clatter of glasses and the clap of dominoes in the bar mingled with the roar of bellows and the musical blows of the hammer on the anvil, the snorts of horses and the hiss of steam when a shoe was plunged into a quenching trough of water to temper it. John Evans had a wide knowledge of the anatomy of the horse and at one time was the only vet in Pontypridd.

The Tredegar Arms was not far from the Fountain and one regular Temperance Society speaker in 1898 often left his meeting there and strode the distance to the pub, then kept by Richard Williams, while beating on a big drum and calling out the drinkers with threats of hell fire. Before his retinue of new followers drifted away they would point accusing fingers at the heathens they saw in the pub windows or would hurl insults at the driver of the Crosswell's beer delivery cart. Meanwhile, some onlookers would pop into the 'jug and bottle' window of the Tredegar for a flagon or two of bitter ale.

Members of the fire brigade enjoyed a drink at the Firemen's Arms at the rear of Turnpike Lane by the Fairfield end of the cattle market and close to their new headquarters in Gas Lane. The Bridge Inn was situated at 1 Berw Road, now part of the new police station site. Just along Berw Road—with its houses once known as Tredegar Street—was the Ruperra Hotel (now the site of Ruperra flats) well remembered by many boxing enthusiasts. James Cook was the landlord in 1879. The pub was rebuilt in the late 1890s and when police visited it one night a constable stood in the newly constructed doorway while a sergeant questioned the landlord about serving drinks after 11 pm. As the sergeant wrote in his notebook, the bar partly emptied when several illicit drinkers felt a sudden need to go out the back. They left the Ruperra quietly one by one through the old front door. The escape route was compromised when one drunk fell into the gutter and started singing a celebrated sospan song.

Across the Old Bridge was the Maltsters Arms. The present Maltsters was built in the late Victorian years and Edward Williams, with his wife Ellen, came as landlord in the 1880s. The eighteenth-century Old Maltsters stood further towards the present-day health centre in grounds opposite the river ford and on the site of a small inn originally named the White Horse Inn—one of two inns in the town of that name, although of different times. From 1809 the Baptists rented a room over the inn brewhouse for their services until Carmel Chapel was built a year later. William Emmanuel in 1851 and John Rees, a hay dealer, were landlords of this Old Maltsters Arms and the licence transferred to Ann Rees about 1875. The pub was famous for its ghost which, like all good pub ghosts, had a fondness for the cellar.

One night, the maid went down the cellar for a jug of ale. She felt a more distinct chill in the cellar than usual; and when she put the candlestick down and started to fill the jug she saw the misty figure of a man standing among the barrels. The maid shrank back and stared wide-eyed at the ghost. Both were apparently stone cold sober. She closed her eyes tightly and then nervously opened them again. But the apparition was still there and she scuttled back up the cellar steps. It was still there on the maid's second visit. She fled once more and refused to go down again on her own. So her mistress went down as well and kept watch at the foot of the cellar steps as candlelight flickered and shone in the brooch pinned to the dress that hung on her bony skeleton. The ghost did not appear.

The next night, after suffering the taunts and laughs of the drinkers in the bar, the maid dared to go down the cellar alone with her jug. The ghost moved towards her and beckoned her close. Something blew the candle out. Trembling, the maid struck a match to relight it. She clasped her hand tightly across her bosom and learned that the unhappy ghost had lost all his money at cock-fighting bouts. He was unlucky at picking winners and eventually lost everything and passed away. He had dieted and dressed many a cockerel and his last act when cock-fighting was made illegal in 1849 had been to hide a set of two-inch spurs in a secret place near a waterfall in the dark, wooded valley of Cwm Pistyll Goleu at Llanwonno. He would be released from his ghostly penance for wicked law-breaking and find eternal rest only when the tiny spurs were retrieved and thrown into the River Taff to rest there for ever. The maid recovered the spurs and threw them from a bridge into the river as the waters rippled over a dancing reflection of the moon. She found the cellar of the Old Maltsters became hushed and still again except for the slow drip, drip of water on the cold flagstones.

The other White Horse was further up Bridge Street by a small humpbacked bridge over the canal. It was a small whitewashed building and a meeting place for local Methodists who used the long room over the brewhouse for their services. It was later used by other denominations and when the Revd Griffith Hughes of Groeswen was preaching there one night the floor gave way and caused utter confusion. William Edwards was landlord of the White Horse in 1852. The pub was converted and extended in the 1890s and became the famous Queens Hotel of William Hinkley. The Queens was demolished in the

1970s—another victim of the progress of the A470 trunk road.

Sandwiched between the Queens Hotel and the Llanover Arms was a beerhouse called the Crown Inn and later Hinkley's Arcade which sold furniture. For eighteen years the Crown was run by Mrs Elizabeth Evans. When she was prosecuted for allowing illegal drinking on a Sunday over Christmas 1900, she happily handed over her 10s fine: she would never open her doors to bona fide travellers who could be allowed drink on a Sunday but preferred only the company of the residents of Feeder Row, the older part of West Street in Trallwn Gardens behind the pub. A lady born in Feeder Row in 1859 remembered as an eight-year-old girl going with her father to the nearby Gwaelod-y-Garth Inn on what was known until recently as the Corn Stores Hill, of which only a part of the original hill now remains.

The Llanover Arms is at the junction of Bridge street and Llanover Street and still serves today. On one side of the whitewashed building a stone platform with steps was constructed from which horses could be mounted and carriages entered; it also had an iron ring fixed to the wall for tethering horses. The pub looked across Ynysangharad Fields which formed part of the Ynysangharad Estate of Benjamin Hall—related through marriage to the Crawshay ironmasters of Cyfarthfa—whose son, also Benjamin, became Lord Llanover. Big Ben, the great bell in the clock tower of the Houses of Parliament at Westminster, was named after (Sir) Benjamin Hall who was the first commissioner of works in 1858 when the bell was cast. David Davies was landlord of the Llanover Arms in 1850 and was followed by many popular hosts through to Charles Ash in 1898.

Ash formerly kept the Ivor Arms further down the street. An alleyway under the pub led to Ivor Court which, with the adjacent Llewellyn Court, squatted on what is now part of the miniature golf course in Ynysangharad Park. All the buildings were demolished in 1936. Landlords in the 1870s and 1880s included Henry Derry and Charles Stream. The facade of the Ivor Arms was renovated in Edwardian years and the work dated 1907, which wrongly suggests that the pub itself was built that year. Brass bands gave concerts in a field behind, which was a popular venue for local sports and fetes and the annual visit of Bostock & Wombwell's menagerie and circus whose horses would parade through the streets drawing gilded chariots escorted by a military band to advertise the presence once again of the show.

Above: Eglwysilan Church *c.* 1900. **Below:** A Victorian print of Penuel chapel and the Fountain, with the entrance to the Town Hall and Pontypridd Market on the right,and the roadway which led to the chapel graveyard. The roadway was roofed in 1929 and is now a fruit, vegetable and flowers area of the market.

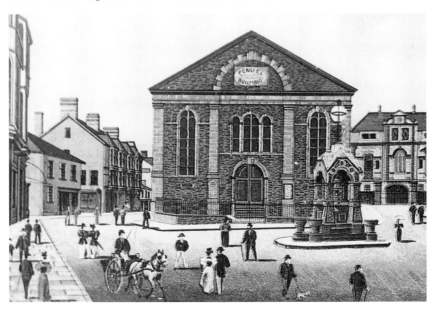

Above: St Illtud's Church, Llantwit Fardre, in 1991. The church was restored in 1854 but the register dates from 1626. **Below:** Glyntaff Crematorium in 1991. The Glyntaff Burial Board was formed in 1871. There were two mortuary chapels, one for the Church of England and one for the Nonconformists.

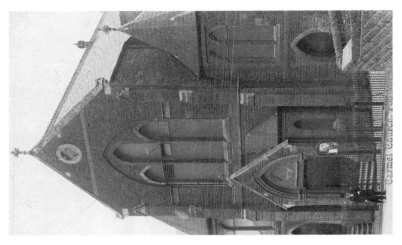

Carmel Chapel, built in 1810.

St Catherine's Church, Pontypridd, built in 1868.

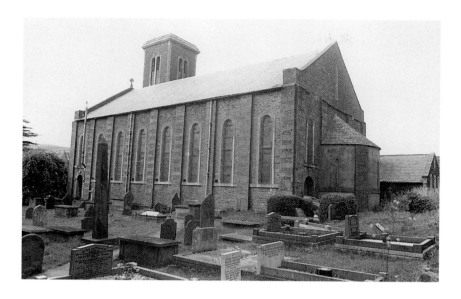

Above: St Mary's Church, Glyntaff, built in the 1830s, in 1991. **Below:** The Llanover Arms at the junction of Bridge Street and Llanover Street, also photographed in 1991. Near the stack of barrels, a stone platform was constructed from which horses could be mounted and carriages entered.

Above: The bandstand in Ynysangharad Park, 1991. In late Victorian days the site of the bandstand was Pontypridd RFC's playing field. **Below:** The Rocking Stone and Stone Circle, Pontypridd Common, 1899.

Above: Hats off to (and worn by) a Victorian married couple. William and Beatrice Fishbourne, latterly of Rhydyfelin. **Below:** Pontypridd Library in 1899.

Above: The Round Houses, Graig-yr-Helfa, Glyntaff. **Below:** The old Ivor Arms Hotel, opened before 1870 in Bridge Street near the present-day Health Centre. The photograph shows its new facade of 1907. The pub and adjacent Ivor Court and Llewellyn Court were demolished in 1936.

Memorial to Evan James and James James.

David Evans, Chairman of Pontypridd UDC.

James James (1832–1902).

Evan James (1809–78).

Above: Morning Star, Graig, *c.* 1899. **Below:** Graig Hotel, *c.* 1899.

Along Ynysangharad Road were the Cable and Anchor and the Kings Head. Sunday drinkers at the Kings Head more than once paid the penalty of a hefty £1 fine after they were spotted in the windows by the local constable alerted to the scene of fighting among the revellers outside the nearby Peasley Carriage Works. The most famous pub in Ynysangharad Road, the Bunch of Grapes, still exists. Tended for many Victorian years by Thomas Allen, the pub was a favourite haunt of smiths employed at Brown Lenox chainworks across the canal who found relief from the heat of their fires in cool quarts of ale. The pub was also the Ynysangharad Brewery Bottling Stores, famous for its fine old bitter beers, ales and stouts, hop bitters and ginger beer. A horse and cart delivered orders to all parts of Pontypridd and some orders were even sent by post. They included a dozen pint bottles of ale and stout for 2s 6d and four-gallon casks at 6s 6d.

A walk across Ynysangharad Fields brought one to the 1897 carriage bridge over the Taff at the rear of the Butchers Arms, renamed the Park Hotel that year. The name 'Butchers Arms Hotel' can still be seen set in stone lettering just below the gable roof of the Midland Bank facing Taff Street. From early in the 1850s the landlord and brewer was John Jones. Edgar Treharne came in the 1890s and his new lodge room, lit by electricity generated in a yard at the rear of the building, was considered to be the finest in the country. The yard (Jacob Studt's field) often filled with people attending the sales of carts and carriages. Pearson's Auction Vans were parked in the yard from 6.30 every evening. The proprietors knew a brisk trade in the auction of watches and crockery which followed free entertainment by jugglers and acrobats and song-and-dance men. Billiards competitions were frequently held at the Butchers Arms—one competitor was a famous Pontypridd personality, Joe Ball, manager of the local Social Club. In later years he ran a billiards and snooker hall with several tables in a room above today's Burton's outfitters.

In Mill Street, the County Hotel was a popular spot for dancing, open banquets on St David's Day, and wedding receptions. John and Rachel Williams kept the Colliers Arms for more than twenty years from the 1860s. The Colliers was demolished some years ago when an arch of Brunel's Taff Vale viaduct over the Rhondda was widened for a one-way road system. The pub was a favourite place for many colliers and on the pavement nearby one 'butty' would often say to another: 'Does geni ddim digon i codi cliciad!' or 'I'm broke—I haven't enough to raise the latch!', only to be shepherded inside the pub to share the pennies or have a debt chalked up 'on the slate' behind the bar for settlement at a more prosperous moment. Just beyond the viaduct, at the foot of Graigwen Hill and the junction with Rhondda Road, the Dynevor Arms stood at the end of a row of houses.

Near Mill Street school was the Welsh Harp: the Victorian pub was not the large Welsh Harp building which was recently renovated and opened as the Millfield Hotel, but a small building some thirty yards further up. The old Welsh Harp was demolished about 1904 when alterations were made to the seven-arch railway viaduct over the Rhondda for the proposed electrification of the Pontypridd to Porth tramline.

Pontypridd High Street led to a cluster of pubs on the Tumble or Station Square. The Victoria, initially named the Victoria and Somerset, was managed for many years from 1850 by Joseph Loxton. It was occupied for a time in recent years by the local Job Centre. The Vic had the notorious Two-Foot-Nine bar. Steps of this height led down to a smoky, seamy bar much frequented by prostitutes of the town and their pursuers. In 1895, Jack Davies was landlord of the Victoria and also proprietor of the Empire Music Hall and Theatre of Varieties, a huge attraction for Victorians, which presented many artistes and acts in what are now called 'good old days' musical shows. The Empire stood at the rear of the Victoria with access through an alleyway, fronted by covered columns on the pavement, beside the former Sketchley Cleaners. The Empire was known earlier as Howard's Hall after proprietor Edward Howard who was landlord of the Victoria in 1880. The Pontypridd Lyric Club often entertained there in 1888 and 1889. In 1897, Monsieur Le Claire's cinématographe was introduced at the Empire. It presented comedy films which lasted only a minute or so but fascinated everyone. Also the magic lantern, which projected images on a small screen from slides, enthralled mainly young local audiences, with compelling titles like 'Bring Your Own Cherries'.

Across the road, part of a building which became the Royal Clarence Theatre in the early 1890s was the Ivy Bush by today's Hooper & Rose jewellers, kept by William Seaton in the 1880s. Further up the High Street and adjoining the theatre was the old Clarence Hotel, a squat building altered in 1912 into the present building. William Jones was landlord of the Clarence in 1871. He was followed for some 25 years from the mid-1870s by John Trenchard of the Royal

Clarence Theatre, and fellow proprietor Tom Jones. One of the apparent attractions of the Clarence Hotel was a tribe of monkeys caged in one corner of the bar. They kept up a tirade of chatter which ceased only when they were blissfully inebriated, a state into which they were quickly encouraged by the droves of drinkers. The Clarence was given a major facelift in 1987 by Whitbread Wales Limited and renamed Angharad's.

Opposite the Clarence, on the site of today's Criterion, was the Bunch of Grapes which was one of the town's busiest pubs. The landlord in the 1890s was John Thomas who also ran the Wheatsheaf in Soar Street. Many of the drunk and disorderly charges brought before the magistrates concerned drinkers thrown out of the Bunch of Grapes or found paralytic on the pavement shortly after leaving the premises. But its terrors did not cool the blood and fire of the staunch Salvationists who carried the *War Cry* there (and to all local pubs) from the 1880s.

Two of the other Victorian pubs on the Tumble are still going. The White Hart, an old commercial hotel and post house kept in 1851 by Thomas Jones when the county court sat there monthly, is popular with young people today as 'The Flicks' discothèque. George Parfitt was the long-serving landlord there and took care of the large billiards room above the bar. The roadway outside was a favourite venue for the Salvation Army band who often played in the light of a large oil lantern fixed to a long pole. Adjoining the White Hart is the Greyhound tended by Thomas Thomas in 1851 and a string of other landlords before David Williams in the 1890s. The Half Moon, which was held under a lease granted in 1847, was sold in 1899 to the Rhondda Brewery Co. for £2,500 and Samuel Stanbury became the landlord. The Half Moon closed in 1989 and was demolished to make way for road improvements.

Opposite the Half Moon the Blue Bell stood in the station yard. Just along Sardis Road was the Prince of Wales and close by was the Castle Hotel. Adjoining the Half Moon and between it and the High Street railway bridge (which was much narrower before 1899 than today) was the Red Lion and Railway Hotel, one of the oldest Pontypridd town licences and in existence in 1833. It was owned by the Taff Vale Railway but the pub failed in 1899 when alterations to the bridge and station, and a declining moral reputation, caused a severe loss of trade. The Red Lion was demolished when part of a five-arched station approach (which started opposite the old R.J. Bown's garage) was erected over it.

On the Tramroad, where the main Pontypridd post office is situated today, was the Lamb Inn (later The Sportsman), kept in 1852 by Evan Davies. There were many other pubs in the immediate vicinity. Prohibition was tried on a Saturday throughout the town when magistrates ordered public houses to close at 2 pm on 6 October 1900. Local newspapers proclaimed the success of the day during which 'there were no drunks, no brawls, no prostitutes, and the starving were fed'. The following week everything returned to its day-long intoxicated, lustful normality.

Glimpses

Pontypridd in the later years of Queen Victoria's reign abounded with quacks promoting their remedies, auctioneers drawing crowds of bargain hunters, and speakers propounding their temperance, religious and other philosophies. Breton onion sellers or 'Shoni onion men' were familiar characters in Taff Street from the 1880s. A muffin-man stood near Market Square and rang his small bell to attract passers-by. On his head he carried a wooden tray of hot muffins covered with green baize cloth to keep them warm. On Good Friday, bakers sold hot cross buns in the streets and shouted the familiar jingle, 'One a penny, two a penny, hot cross buns!' People clustered round Tom Marshman's (old Tom Cockles) cart for bags of cockles. Hot pie shops, fish and chip shops and the chip van outside the Butchers Arms spread their aromas through the town. Gallagher's Oyster Saloon was situated next to the New Inn side of a building which is now the NatWest Bank. Oysters were cheap and were served with lemon slices and hunks of bread and then washed down with a bottle or two of stout.

In the 1880s, John Garett of Foundry Place, Coedpenmaen, could be seen strolling round the town as he sold copies of his twopenny booklet containing his ballad 'The Pontypridd collier in search of his wife'. On summer days, crowds made for the delightful Berw Pool below Coed Craig-yr-Hesg. There were proposals for the area to be attractively laid out. Nothing was done but the Berw remained a popular picnic spot though several swimmers were drowned in the pool. There were suggestions that houses should be built on the Ynysangharad Estate but instead the fields became the Ynysangharad Memorial Park in 1923. There were also proposals to lay out the Common overlooking Pontypridd as a park but they were not acted on.

The Common was a fashionable place for open-air events and was familiar ground for many courting couples. It was usually crowded on warm Sunday evenings when people strolled to the Rocking Stone in their 'Sunday best' after attending church or chapel. The Treforest Corps Salvation Army band regularly played there and preachers drew large crowds. The *Pontypridd Observer* commented on the increasing number of Sunday games played on the Common, such as leap frog, football, and stone and turf slinging—all in Christian Wales. The paper highlighted the action of a Graig-yr-Hesg man who condemned a bunch of children for picking blackberries on a Sunday while he discharged a fusillade of foul language to disperse the damned heathens. Saturday fairs were held at times and the gaily striped drinking booths, set as close as pages in a Bible, overflowed with custom.

The Rocking Stone *(Y Maen Chwyf)* is of local pennant stone and may have been deposited on the Common as a result of glacial action. It is balanced on a natural rock base and weighs about 9½ tons. The stone is now difficult to move but at one time could be rocked easily by exerting pressure on its south side. The Druidism of Pontypridd is of early nineteenth-century creation and the writer Morien related that Iolo Morganwg (Edward Williams) presided at a ceremony held at the Rocking Stone in 1815 and at several others subsequently.

Taliesin ab Iolo Morganwg presided over a Gorsedd at the Rocking Stone in September 1834. The Druids afterwards retired to the house of Gwilym Morganwg which formed part of the New Inn Hotel where the bard was landlord at the time. A serpent of standing stones surrounds the Rocking Stone. It is made up of two concentric circles joined to a winding avenue of stones ending in a small circle that has the two eyes of the serpent. It is believed that Evan Davies created the serpent in 1850. Known as Myfyr Morganwg, Evan Davies settled in Pontypridd as a watchmaker in 1844 and succeeded Taliesin as Chief Druid in 1847. Myfyr won the chair at Pontypridd in 1853 for the Welsh ode *The Sacred Circles of the Bards*, and held Druidic ceremonies at the Rocking Stone until 1878. Dr William Price, who disputed the title of Archdruid of Wales with Myfyr, took an interest in Druidism in Pontypridd and claimed that he had discovered the key to the secrets of the Druids. He did not, however, perform Druidic rites himself at the Rocking Stone but had, in his own words, 'only chanted a song of the primitive bard to the moon'.

The town enjoyed a wide range of sport: Pontypridd had a strong and stylish cricket team in 1897 when the Glamorgan Cricket League was established. In 1899 the Pontypridd Wheelers Cycle Club had 43 members with headquarters at the Llanover Arms. Just opposite the pub, near the chainworks entrance to Ynysangharad Fields, the new tennis courts then situated there drew many players. Treforest had its own tennis club at Taff Vale Park and its own cycling club which often organised picnic runs to Hensol Castle and other places in the Vale of Glamorgan. There was a shooting club which used a rifle range alongside the Barry Railway line at Hopkinstown, and another at Cilfynydd which set up its targets in a quarry below Oaklands. Their activities and aims were closely monitored by members of the several homing pigeon societies in the district.

Boxing thrived in the town and on Monday 23 August 1897 Pontypridd boxing fans packed the trains and horse-trams from Pontypridd to the Rhondda to visit a boxing booth at Pandy Field near the Square in Tonypandy. A fight with gloves had been promoted by a travelling showman and hundreds of spectators cheered on the two rugged contestants. After eight rounds the referee declared a winner, but four more rounds were fought. The loser died in the night.

The two strongest rugby clubs in the district were Pontypridd and Cilfynydd. Pontypridd RFC, with its ground now at Sardis Road, was formed in 1875–76 and was known as Pontypridd Football Club through the Victorian and Edwardian years. Its first home ground was at Taff Vale Park off the Broadway; later the club played at the Peoples' Park at Millfield and afterwards at Ynysangharad Fields on a pitch set out where the present-day bandstand is situated. The club was one of the ten represented at a meeting at the Tenby Hotel in Swansea in 1880 when the Welsh Rugby Union was formed.

It is probable that Cilfynydd RFC, which still plays on the old Welfare Grounds alongside the village, was formed shortly after the sinking of the Albion Colliery in 1886. There is mention of Cilfynydd RFC Harlequins from 1888 to 1891. The *South Wales Daily News* of 18 December 1893 records a win by Cilfynydd over Loudons, a Cardiff side, at Sophia Gardens. There is record of a successful 1899–1900 season for the club with fixtures with a dozen or more local and Rhondda clubs. Cilfynydd RFC chose to celebrate its official 75th anniversary during the 1977–78 season to mark club membership of the Welsh Rugby Union in 1902.

In September 1899 Miss Clara Thomas of Llwynmadoc converted Gelliwastad House on Gelliwastad Road into a Workmen's Institute with reading rooms, billiards rooms, skittle alley and a place where men could sit and smoke and have a meal but no intoxicating drinks. A lawn, today a car park, was used for playing bowls and quoits. A library and reading room, known as the Pontypridd Literary Institute, was established in 1860. It was situated first near the Fountain in Taff Street and later in Market Street. John Sharp was the librarian in 1871—when the library already had a stock of a thousand books—and David Roderick was librarian for many years afterwards. The present Free Library (recently extensively renovated) was built in Gelliwastad Grove in 1890 at a cost of £2,000. George Hughes was the librarian in 1895 and the library soon had 2,000 books but, without an assistant, the librarian was unable to catalogue them. There were workmen's institute libraries at Cilfynydd, Treforest and Trehafod by 1899 when the Pontypridd Library had 4,000 books and 2,900 keen borrowers.

The Young Men's Christian Association opened a branch in Pontypridd on 23 March 1899 next to Daniel Arnott's chemist shop at 35a Taff Street. The YMCA made good progress in the town and later held their meetings at the Gelliwastad Institute. The *Pontypridd Observer* was glad to note that the YMCA had demonstrated that cycling clubs could be run successfully without desecration of the Sabbath. The present large YMCA building at the junction of Crossbrook Street and Taff Street was opened in September 1910. In April 1899, a women's branch, the YWCA, was formed in the town and held Bible classes at Hopkin Morgan's restaurant in Taff Street. Young women joined sewing circles and embroidery classes. They made samplers embroidered with their own names and ages and with patterns and texts as specimens to show the various stitches they had learned.

Anglican services were first held at Pontypridd in licensed rooms in Morgan Street and then in a building in Temperance Place off Gas Lane. The first church in the town was St Mary's at Glyntaff, built in the 1830s at a cost of £2,000. The register dates from 1834 and the first service was held in 1841. St Catherine's in Pontypridd was built of local stone in 1868 at a cost of £7,000, which was given, together with the site, by the Thomas family of Ystrad Mynach and Llwynmadoc. The north aisle was added in 1885. The tower has a spire 162ft high and contained a peal of eight bells and the famous four-sided clock. Miss Clara Thomas designed, worked and presented the altar cloth to the church. The vicarage was built in 1890 and the parish rooms were built in 1891. The Revd J.G. Griffiths was the vicar in 1898.

St David's, Gyfeillon, was opened in 1851, while the parish church of St Illtud's in Llantwit Fardre (Llanilltud Faerdref) was restored in 1854, although the register dates from 1626. Other churches established in Pontypridd in the 1890s included St Matthew's, Coedpenmaen; St Mark's, Pwllgwaun; St John's, Graig; and St Luke's, Cilfynydd, built as a chapel of ease to Eglwysilan in 1893. The church at Eglwysilan has inspired local people with its teachings for a thousand years: the nave dates from the late eleventh or twelfth century although it is believed that there was a Christian foundation on its lonely site from the sixth century. St Ilan was probably a Celtic saint but there is an opinion that the parish is properly Eglwys-Elian. Another opinion holds that the church was dedicated to Elen (or Helen) Deg, the daughter of Morgan Mwynfawr, with the derivation supported by the fact that in the parish is the hamlet of Cwmheldeg or Cwm-elen-deg, 'fair Elen's valley', some miles along the mountain road above Cilfynydd. The parish churches of Llanfabon and Llanwonno are also ancient.

After Carmel Baptist Chapel was built on Graigwen Hill in 1810 the Dissenters, who from the seventeenth century refused to conform to the teachings of the Church of England, set up many places of worship in Pontypridd. In late Victorian years there were more than forty Nonconformist chapels throughout the district for Baptist, Congregational, Methodist, Wesleyan, Independent and other Protestant denominations. The Roman Catholic Church built in 1857 at Treforest was dedicated to St Dubricius and is known today as St Dyfrig's. The Revd Father Michael Joseph McManus was the priest in 1895 and for many years afterwards.

Local choirs performed at the Empire Music Hall. Pontypridd United Choir was always an attraction there. In 1896 Pontypridd had a 100-voice male choir, conducted by David E. Phillips, which often gave concerts at the New Town Hall. About this time there were male voice choirs in Cilfynydd, Rhydyfelin, and Treforest, which also had a ladies chorus. The local post office had its own choir and the Chainworks Choir often assembled at the chainworks chapel in Ynysangharad Road. The Treorchy Male Voice Choir, the pride of the valleys, was engaged to sing before Queen Victoria. There were many brass and silver bands: the local Volunteer and the Temperance Movement bands competed enthusiastically with bands from the Town, Trallwn and Penyrhiw, and with those of the Lewis Merthyr, Great Western, and Albion collieries. In June 1899 more than thirty bands entered a contest held at Taff Vale Park.

The great Welsh hymn *Cwm Rhondda* was first sung in Capel Rhondda Welsh Baptist, Hopkinstown, in 1907. It was originally called *Rhondda* and was written by John Hughes, a colliery clerk from Tonteg, for a Cymanfa Ganu at the chapel that year. He was inspired by Dr Joseph Parry—famed for his writing of many hymn tunes, songs, oratorios, cantatas and operas—whose musical ability blossomed while he worked at the Pennsylvania Ironworks in the United States. The works of Dr Parry were regularly performed in Pontypridd and the districts, particularly at Cilfynydd, a village still proud of its musical heritage today whose streets and primary school reared and nurtured two internationally renowned opera stars: Sir Geraint Evans and Stuart Burrows. Pontypridd takes pride, too, in the performances of its male voice choir—Cor Meibion Pontypridd, and in the Pontypridd Choral Society and the voices of Gillian Humphreys, Beverley Humphreys, Tom Jones, Iris Williams and others.

At the National Eisteddfod of Wales held in Pontypridd in August 1893 a blacksmith named Griffiths Rhys Jones (Caradoc), who had led a choir of 500 voices to success at the Crystal Palace in London in 1872, conducted a large choir which rehearsed at the parish rooms behind 'Brynhyfryd' in Courthouse Street. Hundreds of Graig residents thronged the street on the warm summer nights to enjoy and applaud the voices. Tom Stephens, a local musician who died at Church Village in 1906, conducted the Rhondda Glee Society which won the male voice section at Pontypridd and also first prize at the Chicago World Eisteddfod in the United States.

Hen Wlad Fy Nhadau

Evan James, born in Caerphilly in 1809, came to Pontypridd in 1844 with his wife and their son, James James, to take over 'Ty'r Ffatri', a small woollen factory in Mill Street. Evan James was a thoughtful and religious man known to his contemporaries by his bardic name Ieuan ab Iago. He wrote several pieces of patriotic poetry and was rarely without his slate on which he jotted down phrases and ideas. James James loved music and was an accomplished harpist and singer. Over the years he composed a number of songs for the verses written by his father. In 1910 Taliesin, the son of James James, wrote to his deceased father's harp teacher, John Crockett of Pontypridd. Before Taliesin was the original manuscript of a melody dated January 1856. Late one afternoon, Taliesin wrote, James James had walked up Mill Street and Rhondda Road and had composed the melody as he strolled along.

He returned to the factory house and asked his father if he would write some verses to fit the melody. 'Fetch your harp, James', his father said, and while young James played sweetly on the harp Evan took up his slate which hung by the side of his high-backed chair close to the fireplace. In minutes, he wrote the first verse of *Glan Rhondda*. Taliesin went on to write that James James sang the words as he accompanied himself on the harp. His mother returned from evening service at Carmel Baptist Chapel nearby and reprimanded her son for desecrating the Sabbath by playing the harp. He protested: 'Ond Mam, Brenin Dafydd canodd y delyn.' His mother remembered then that the biblical King David played the harp, and she had given her blessing. Evan James wrote the second and third verses of *Glan Rhondda* the next day.

The original manuscript of what was later called *Hen Wlad Fy Nhadau* was lodged in the National Library of Wales at Aberystwyth. The words are as sung today but the music differs in several ways: for example, the first eight bars of the chorus have been cut to five. The tune has been translated into Irish, Gaelic, Manx, Cornish and Breton to become a Pan-Celtic anthem. When Evan James died on 30 September 1878 his armchair was given as a token to a friend of the family. Her granddaughter, Mrs M. Gray of Pontypridd, presented the chair to Pontypridd Library in the 1950s. James James helped his father in the weaving business in Pontypridd for several years before going to live in Mountain Ash. He died in Aberdare on 11 January 1902.

Sixteen-year-old Elizabeth John gave the first public performance of the song at the Calvinistic Methodist Chapel, Maesteg, in January 1856. James James sang it at a Pontypridd eisteddfod in 1859 when Thomas Llewellyn put the song in notation form for inclusion in his prize-winning repertoire of Welsh tunes performed at a Llangollen national eisteddfod. The adjudicator John Owen (Owain Alaw) was impressed and used the composition in 1860 in his *Gems of Welsh Melodies*. It was sung at the Bangor National Eisteddfod in 1874 and frequently at eisteddfodau and concerts until 1880 when it was generally accepted, and in 1899 officially recognised, as the Welsh National Anthem.

Rhys Morgan, a Pontypridd schoolmaster, initiated a memorial fund to honour the composers. On 23 July 1930 Lord Treowen, watched by some 10,000 people, unveiled the memorial in Ynysangharad Park. Designed by Sir William Goscombe John, the memorial consists of two bronze figures, a woman representing poetry and a male harpist representing music, and is set on a plinth of blue pennant stone from Graig-yr-Hesg quarry. The stone bears a medallion of father and son and an inscription in Welsh and English.

In memory of
Evan James
and
James James
1809–1878
1832–1902
father and son
of Pontypridd
who inspired by a deep and tender
love of their native land united
poetry and song and gave to Wales
her national hymn *Hen Wlad Fy Nhadau*

At the unveiling ceremony, Taliesin James played the anthem on his harp and afterwards a procession went to Carmel Chapel graveyard where Evan James was buried. When the chapel was demolished in recent years and Plas Carmel Flats built on the site, the remains of Evan James were reburied at the Ynysangharad Park Memorial. *Hen Wlad Fy Nhadau* stays dear to the descendants of the Pontypridd Victorians—and to all the people of the Welsh nation whose hearts the anthem has stirred for a century. May it endure. *O bydded i'r hen iaith barhau.*

Epilogue

The sixty-year reign of Queen Victoria ended when she died on Tuesday, 22 January 1901. News of her approaching end brought grief throughout Britain. Most of its citizens had never known a time without Queen Victoria as monarch. Memorial services were held on the following Sunday in all churches and chapels in Pontypridd.

On the day of the queen's funeral, Saturday 2 February 1901, window blinds were drawn throughout the bitterly cold town and district. Shops and offices closed and the pubs shut their doors for part of the day. Pontypridd was hushed except for the solemn tolling of a bell in St Catherine's to where Supt Cole and a line of constables escorted local dignitaries for a memorial service. At the church gates the Volunteer and Great Western Colliery bands played Chopin's *Funeral March* and buglers sounded the *Last Post*.

The proclamation of Edward VII as king was made from the steps of Penuel Chapel in Taff Street at 2 pm on Wednesday 6 February. It was read in English by Hugh Bramwell, chairman of the urban district council in 1900–01, and in Welsh by Hopkin Morgan, chairman 1901–02.

Later, from his home near St Catherine's, Councillor Hopkin Morgan looked out towards the mountain slopes of Eglwysilan darkened beneath a sky stained wine red and purple by the last embers of the day. He had seen vast changes in Pontypridd through the Victorian years. He considered them in a rushing tide of recollection and pondered what the future held for his beloved town in the new century ahead. In the morning, shafts of sunlight shone brightly through the early mists as Pontypridd, with generally an enviable community spirit, stepped forward into a new Edwardian age.

Appendix

Pontypridd's Victorian Pubs and Inns

Albion Hotel, Cilfynydd Road, Cilfynydd

Baileys Arms, Graig-yr-Helfa, Glyntaff
Ballers Arms, Tram Road, Treforest
Bassett Arms, Merthyr Road, Pontshon-norton
Blue Bell Inn, Station Yard, Tumble, Pontypridd
Bonvilston Hotel, Coedpenmaen Road, Coedpenmaen
Boot Inn, Tram Road, Tumble, Pontypridd
Bridge Inn, Berw Road, Pontypridd
Bridge Inn, Bridge Street, Treforest
Bridge-end Inn, Gyfeillon Road, Gyfeillon
Bunch of Grapes, High Street, Tumble, Pontypridd (Criterion)
Bunch of Grapes, Ynysangharad Road, Pontypridd
Bush Inn, Main Road, Llantwit Fardre
Bush Inn, Park Street, Treforest (RAFA Club)
Butchers Arms, Taff Street, Pontypridd (Park Hotel)

Cable and Anchor, Ynysangharad Road, Pontypridd
Cambrian, Treforest
Carpenters Arms, Efail Isaf, Llantwit Fardre
Carpenters Arms, High Street, Graig
Castle Hotel, Tram Road, Pontypridd
Castle Inn, Treforest
Castle Ivor, Rhondda Road, Hopkinstown
Central Hotel, Central Square, Trallwn
Cilfynydd Inn, Cilfynydd Road, Cilfynydd
Clarence Hotel, High Street, Tumble Pontypridd (Angharad's)
Colliers Arms, Llantwit Fardre
Colliers Arms, Nantgarw
Colliers Arms, Eirw, Trehafod

Colliers Arms, Mill Street, Pontypridd
Colliers Arms, Upper Boat
Colliers Delight, High Street, Graig (Globe)
Commercial Hotel, Cilfynydd Road, Cilfynydd (Spite)
Commercial Hotel, Forest Road, Treforest (Otley Arms)
County Hotel, Mill Street, Pontypridd
Criterion: see Bunch of Grapes, Pontypridd
Cross Inn, High Street, Graig
Cross Inn, Main Road, Church Village
Cross Keys, Cardiff Road, Nantgarw
Cross Keys, Tram Road, Tumble, Pontypridd
Crown Inn, Bridge Street, Pontypridd
Crown Inn, Cardiff Road, Rhydyfelin
Crown Inn, Fothergill Street, Treforest
Crown Inn, Main Road, Llantwit Fardre

Danygraig Arms, Tram Road, Treforest
Duke of Bridgewater Arms, Pentrebach Road, Glyntaff
Duffryn Arms, Rhydyhelyg, Llantwit Fardre
Dyffryn Arms, Cardiff Road, Rhydyfelin (Jubilee)
Dynevor Arms, Rhondda Road, Pontypridd

Fair Oak, Eirw, Trehafod
Farmers Arms, Llanfabon
Farmers Arms, Pentrebach Road, Glyntaff
Farmers Arms, St Illtyd's Road, Church Village
Farmers Hotel, Trehafod Road, Gyfeillon
Farriers Arms, Llanganna, Graig
Firemens Arms, River Street (Rear), Pontypridd
Fox and Hounds, Llantwit Fardre

Fox and Hounds, Cardiff Road, Upper Boat

Fox and Hounds, Llantrisant Road, Graig

Forest Hotel (Cot), Wood Road, Treforest

Glanrhondda Hotel, Gyfeillon

Globe Hotel: see Colliers Delight, Graig

Glyntaff Inn, Tram Road, Treforest

Graig Hotel, Llantrisant Road, Graig

Great Western Hotel, Gyfeillon

Green Meadow, High Street, Graig

Greyhound Hotel, Llanfabon (Llanfabon Hotel)

Greyhound Hotel, Tram Road, Tumble, Pontypridd

Greyhound Hotel, Tonteg

Greyhound Hotel, Park Street, Treforest

Griffin, Tram Road, Treforest

Gwaelod-y-Garth Inn, Corn Stores Hill, Pontypridd

Half Moon Hotel, High Street, Tumble, Pontypridd

Hawthorn Inn, Cardiff Road, Hawthorn

Hewitts Arms, Llantrisant Road, Penycoedcae

Hollybush Hotel, Main Road, Church Village

Hollybush Hotel, Tymawr Road, Hopkinstown

Horse and Groom, High Street, Graig

Ivor Arms, Bridge Street, Pontypridd

Ivy Bush, High Street, Tumble Pontypridd

Kings Head, Ynysangharad Road, Pontypridd

Lamb and Flag, Pentrebach Road Glyntaff

Lamb Inn, Tram Road, Tumble, Pontypridd (Sportsman)

Llanbradach Arms, Machine Bridge, Glyntaff

Llanover Arms, Bridge Street, Pontypridd

Maltsters Arms, Bridge Street, Pontypridd

Maltsters Arms, Ebenezer Street Rhydyfelin

Merlin Hotel, Pwllgwaun Road, Pwllgwaun

Morning Star, Llantrisant Road, Graig

Moulders Arms, Upper Boat

Newbridge Arms, Foundry Road, Coedpenmaen

New Inn, Main Road, Llantwit Fardre

New Inn, Cardiff Road, Rhydyfelin

New Inn Hotel, Taff Street, Pontypridd

Old House at Home, Treforest

Park Hotel: see Butchers Arms, Pontypridd

Park Inn, Treforest

Pelican Inn, Gellidawel, Rhydyfelin (Little Apple)

Plough Inn, Cardiff Road, Rhydyfelin

Prince of Wales, Tram Road, Tumble, Pontypridd

Queen Adelaide, Fothergill Street, Treforest

Queens Head, Llantrisant Road, Penycoedcae

Queens Hotel, Llantwit Fardre

Queens Hotel, Bridge Street, Pontypridd

Railway Inn, Llantwit Fardre

Railway Inn, Tram Road, Treforest (The Golden Age)

Red Cow, Rhondda Road, Hopkinstown

Red Lion Hotel, High Street, Tumble, Pontypridd

Rhondda Railway Inn, High Street, Graig

Rhydyfelin Inn, Cardiff Road, Rhydyfelin

Rhydyhelyg, Llantwit Fardre

Richards Arms, Cilfynydd Road, Cilfynydd

Rickards Arms, Park Street, Treforest

Rising Sun, Treforest

Rockingstone Inn, Common, Pontypridd

Rock Inn, Nantgarw

Rolling Mill Inn, Rickard Street steps
    Pontypridd
Rose and Crown, Eglwysilan
Rose and Crown, High Street, Graig
Royal Oak, Rhondda Road, Hopkinstown
Royal Oak, Merthyr Road, Pontshonnor-
    ton
Royal Oak, Treforest
Ruperra Arms, Berw Road, Pontypridd

Salmon Arms, Llantwit Road, Treforest
Ship Brewery, Llantwit Fardre
Sportsman: see Lamb Inn, Pontypridd
Star Inn, Nantgarw
Swan, Treforest

Taff Vale Hotel, High Street, Graig
Three Horse Shoes, High Street, Graig
Three Horse Shoes, Llantwit Road, Ton-
    teg
Tredegar Arms, Taff Street, Pontypridd
Trehafod Hotel, Rhondda Road, Trehafod

Tymawr Hotel, Pantygraigwen, Graigwen
Union Bridge Inn, Canal Place, Ponty-
    pridd
Upper Boat Inn, Cardiff Road, Upper
    Boat

Vaughan Arms, Eirw, Trehafod
Victoria and Somerset, High Street,
    Tumble, Pontypridd
Volunteers, Tram Road, Tumble, Ponty-
    pridd

Welsh Harp, Mill Street, Pontypridd
Wheatsheaf, Soar Street, Graig
White Cross Inn, Groeswen, Eglwysilan
White Hart Hotel, High Street, Tumble
    Pontypridd
White Horse Inn, Bridge Street, Ponty-
    pridd

Ynysybwl Inn, Old Ynysybwl, Ynysybwl

There were other pubs not listed above around Pontypridd in this period, including short-lived beerhouses. In 1900, canal boatmen often used Clayton's Bar if the nearby Bunch of Grapes in Ynysangharad Road was packed. Other beerhouses included the Bird in the Bush and the Eagle Inn, which was very likely part of a provisions store in the town in 1877 called the Golden Eagle. There is mention of The Rifleman although this may be an alternative name for the Volunteers on the Tumble. The Glyncoch Inn on the road from Pontypridd to Ynysybwl was known in Edwardian days and was possibly a Victorian beerhouse.

Note on Sources

Barrie, D.S.M., *The Taff Vale Railway* (Oakwood Press, 1962).

Barrie, D.S.M., *The Barry Railway* (Oakwood Press, 1962).

Stewart Williams' Glamorgan Historian (Barry, Stewart Williams, 1963–).

Glamorgan County History. Vol. 5. Industrial Glamorgan 1700–1970 (Glamorgan County History Trust, 1980).

Hudson, Kenneth, *Industrial Archaeology* (John Baker, 1963).

Rees, D. Morgan, *Industrial Archaeology of Wales* (Newton Abbot, David & Charles, 1975).

Nance, E. Morton, *The Pottery and Porcelain of Swansea and Nantgarw* (B.T. Batsford, 1942).

Wills, Geoffrey, *English Pottery and Porcelain* (Guiness Signatures, 1969).

Burton, William, *History of English Porcelain* (EP Publishing, 1972).

Addis, John P., *The Crawshay Dynasty* (University of Wales Press, 1957).

Andrews, John F., *Keep Moving. The Story of Solomon Andrews and his Family* (Barry, Stewart Williams, 1976).

Charles, John, *Pontypridd Historical Handbook* (Glamorgan Times, 1921).

Lewis, E.D., *The Rhondda Valleys* (Phoenix House, 1959).

Evans, E.W., *The Miners of South Wales* (University of Wales Press, 1961).

Arnot, R. Page, *Glowyr de Cymru. A History of the South Wales Miners' Federation (1897–1914* (George Allen & Unwin, 2 vols., 1967–76).

Documents and records, Pontypridd and Abercynon GWR stations, 1943.

Documents and Records, A.G. Gilbertson and R.J. Richardson, Directors at Brown Lenox Chainworks, Pontypridd, 1954.

Pontypridd Almanac (Pontypridd Library, Various volumes).

Glamorgan Police Magazine (South Wales Police Museum, Various volumes).

HM Inspector of Mines, *Report on the Albion Colliery Explosion* (1894).

Roskill, J., *Report of the Albion Colliery Explosion* (1894) (Author was counsel for the Home Secretary).

Retired and working miners of the Albion Colliery, notes from 1952–6.

Various issues of the *Pontypridd Observer, South Wales Echo, Western Mail* and other newspapers in Pontypridd and Cardiff libraries.

Documents, magazines, directories, programmes and minute books in the Local Collection, Pontypridd Library.

Information gathered from visits to the Museum of Welsh Life, St Fagans; National Museum & Gallery of Wales, Cardiff; Welsh Industrial and Maritime Museum, Cardiff; South Wales Police Museum, Bridgend; South Wales Miners' Library, Swansea; Historical and Cultural Centre, Pontypridd; and other places of historical interest in Wales.

Index